THE LIBRARY INTERNET TRAINER'S TOOLKIT

Michael T. Stephens
adapted by
Phil Bradley

**Library Association Publishing
London**

Neal-Schuman NetGuide Series

**Neal-Schuman Publishers, Inc.
New York   London**

Contents

Preface

The Library Internet Trainer's Toolkit includes everything you need to present 12 ready-to-go Internet programs that have been tested and used successfully in a variety of instructional settings. By combining the contents of the CD-ROM—more than four hundred slides, accompanying scripts, directions, handouts, and fliers—with the flexibility of the Microsoft PowerPoint software, you can easily customize, update, and tailor the slides and scripts for your own library's needs and interests. With the CD-ROM and the detailed scripts and step-by-step instructions provided in this manual, librarians have everything needed to jump-start their own Internet training programme or add to an existing one.

My work developing public training programmes at the St. Joseph County Public Library (SJCPL) in South Bend, Indiana, helped create the foundation for *The Library Internet Trainer's Toolkit*. There is a great need to provide librarians and their patrons with useful and comprehensive instruction to master the challenges of the computer revolution and cyberspace. Not very long ago, many librarians, trustees, and government officials questioned the value of teaching the Internet to the information professional and to the public. In a short time, the Web became an essential tool to locate all kinds of information. Whether they wanted official government documents or the cast list of *The Poseidon Adventure*, everyone got online. Effective reference librarians often had to learn to shift gears quickly. One patron's question might send you searching for a fact in a well-worn copy of a print encyclopedia, then searching further in a World Wide Web subject list with potentially useful links to hundreds of Web pages.

Libraries have naturally become a focal point for access to technology with the dawn of the Internet age and the ubiquity of the computer. Librarians, in turn, have assumed the expanding role of trainers and instructors—presenting programmes on the Internet, electronic database searching, online catalogues, and many other technology-related topics. Increasingly, library users expect and even demand training and instruction.

Librarians face public demand for both information and information skills. Technology has come to the rescue with software tools such as PowerPoint and Word. These user-friendly programs have brought about their own instructional innovations by allowing librarians to create and present classes and lectures, hands-on demos, and special topic explorations. *The Library Internet Trainer's Toolkit* can help you meet the new demands of librarianship and meet the needs of your patrons in various ways.

The 12 modules of *The Library Internet Trainer's Toolkit* can be presented in order over the course of a year or in any manner that suits your library. Any of these modules can be presented on its own, combined with others, or presented as the first of a two-part session, where the second half is devoted to hands-on experience or a live online demonstration.

The first four modules offer a logical progression: from a general introduction to computers through navigating and searching the Internet to evaluating Web sites. You might present them at your library as a four-week seminar. Promote it as "Computers and the Internet University," "Learn to Surf the Net," or anything catchy that will create interest in the modules as a series. Use the included handouts and promotional fliers to ensure a successful programme. Modules 5 to 12 cover many of the fascinating areas of the Internet that people are eager to explore. They are stand-alone classes that you can present in any order that works for your library. If you have already begun a technology training programme, you can use these modules to expand it with minimal prep time.

WHAT'S IN EACH MODULE?

Each module in *The Library Internet Trainer's Toolkit* contains four sections. It begins with an introduction, a list of skills the workshop attendees will gain, and tips to make the presentation effective and fun. The presentation of the slides and script complete the module. The dozen modules offer a great range of informative and entertaining issues that patrons are certain to find interesting. They are as follows:

Introducing the Personal Computer

This module introduces the audience to the personal computer and defines much of the jargon associated with it. A fun class for new computer owners and curious library patrons, this module sets the stage for your technology training efforts by establishing a strong foundation.

Navigating the Internet and the World Wide Web

This module offers the basics of the Internet and specifically the World Wide Web. A bit of history, some defined terms, and an explanation of the Internet as a community and information tool highlight this presentation.

Searching the World Wide Web

This module introduces the ins and outs of locating information on the Web. Portals, subject lists, and search engines are defined and discussed. The module is highlighted by an examination of the Open Directory Project and Google.

Evaluating Web Sites

How can users tell what Web sites offer reliable or correct information? This module offers a set of tips and tools to evaluate Web information, including short quizzes that test your audience's knowledge in some fun and interesting ways.

Using E-mail and WWW E-mail Services

Many people come to the library to get access to the Web and e-mail. This module introduces the basics of e-mail as well as an examination of Web-based services that provide free e-mail.

Shopping the World Wide Web—The Internet Consumer Guide

This module explores the popular world of online shopping, defining pertinent terms and examining security issues. Seven habits of effective shoppers round out this class.

Planning and Maintaining a Web Site for Small Businesses, Organizations, or Personal Use

Designed for the library user interested in developing a Web site for an organization, small business, or for personal use, this module includes the basics of hypertext markup language, Web design considerations, establishing domain names, and exploring content issues.

Exploring Internet Video and Audio

For the curious, this module addresses current trends in viewing or listening to multimedia content on the Web. A tutorial on MP3 files and recording CDs closes the module.

Chatting on the Internet

This module introduces Internet-based chat options and the culture of chatting. Definitions and discussions of terms and "chatiquette" round out the presentation.

Surfing Safe! Children and Their Parents on the World Wide Web

Designed for parents and older children, this module examines the benefits of children using the Web and includes safe surfing tips from experts. Useful guidelines from author Larry Magid and the American Library Association make this an informative presentation.

Selling and Saving: Exploring WWW Auctions

Library users are intrigued by eBay™. This module describes what it's like to participate in an online auction at a site like eBay™ or Yahoo!. Tips for buyers and sellers offer something for everyone in the audience.

Picturing the Digital Camera Revolution

Everyone wants to learn how to send and receive photographs, making this one of the most popular of the modules at my library! It explains how a digital camera works, what to look for when purchasing, and what options are available on the Web for storage and printing.

Be sure to read the following section called "How to Use This Toolkit" for detailed instructions on how to customize the slide presentations, scripts, handouts, and fliers for your individual needs and purpose. The number of changes you make to the material to customize the modules is entirely up to you. *The Library Internet Trainer's Toolkit* is designed as a starting point of a learning process limited only by your own interests and creativity. PowerPoint presentations are a terrific tool that librarians enjoy designing and presenting. Patrons appreciate the added effort, the user-friendly approach and the multimedia aspect of the show. I trust you will agree that these presentations can become some of the more exciting, interesting, and engaging forms of group instruction in your library.

Preface to the UK edition

I was delighted to be given the opportunity of anglicizing *The Library Internet Trainer's Toolkit*, since I believe that it will be a valuable addition to any library that has a responsibility for training its users – whoever they happen to be. Taking another author's text and changing it is always an interesting challenge, because you want to ensure that the flavour and enthusiasm remain the same, while making the book easily readable by a British audience. In this instance, it was not a difficult job, since only minor amendments were required.

For those readers who have an interest in such things, I replaced obvious American terms and phrases (such as garage sale) with British terms (i.e. car-boot sale). I changed the prices of items, both to turn them into a sterling price and to update them slightly. I also replaced URLs linking to American sites with those more appropriate for a British audience. However, I left some URLs as they were if they referred to a global resource, or if they made a a very specific point in the training session.

I hope that my alterations will make the book slightly easier for a British audience to use, while keeping the original author's obvious interest and enthusiasm for his subject clear for all to see.

PHIL BRADLEY

How to Use This Toolkit

The Library Internet Trainer's Toolkit will help you save time by providing the basics and letting you customize the presentations to suit your particular needs. Using the *Toolkit* and personalizing presentations is simple. Copy the module presentation to your hard drive, edit it in PowerPoint, and practice with the scripts provided. Copy the script files to your hard drive and edit them in Word or another word-processing program. To present any of the 12 modules, your library will need a computer attached to some type of projection device and a meeting room to use to give the presentation.

You'll be surprised at how easy is to turn these modules into an exciting feature of your library. Just keep the following design and instructions in mind:

CD-ROM COMPONENTS

The Library Internet Trainer's Toolkit CD-ROM contains the 12 modules, each in their own directories. Each contains:

- the PowerPoint slides
- a script for the workshop saved as a Microsoft Word document
- a script for the workshop saved as a text file for use with other word-processing programs

Other files on the CD-ROM of *The Library Internet Trainer's Toolkit* contain:

- the handouts for the workshops
- the fliers to promote the workshops

- the images used in the presentations.
- the movies for optional use in two of the modules.

POWERPOINT FILES

The directory of each module contains the PowerPoint presentation. It can be opened and viewed on any PC or Macintosh with either Microsoft PowerPoint (included in packages like Microsoft Office 2000) or with the free PowerPoint viewer software available at *www.microsoft.com.*

The PowerPoint presentations are ready-to-go: transitions, builds, and animated effects are set in each module. Although sound effects are available in PowerPoint, I have found them to be frustrating to an audience if not amplified correctly during the presentation. I have not inserted sound effects in the builds and animations in the *Toolkit.* Feel free to do so according to your preference and the capability of your presentation equipment to amplify sound.

Once saved to your hard drive, these presentations can be changed and edited extensively or with only minor changes. You can delete points, add new ones, and customize each module. In fact, many of the slides on the enclosed CD-ROM contain instructions for the insertion of your name, your library's name or URL, and more.

Backgrounds, colour schemes, slide designs, and clip-art can also be manipulated to customize each module. Exchange your own digital pictures or library-related art for the photos or art included in the modules. Editing on the slide master level in PowerPoint allows you to include your library's name on each slide.

For more on working with PowerPoint, visit the Microsoft Web page or take a look at *Using Microsoft PowerPoint: A How-To-Do-It Manual for Librarians,* published by Neal-Schuman, 1998, or other books you have in your collection on using PowerPoint.

Note: The Toolkit modules were created on an iMac DV SE and a Powerbook G3 computer with Microsoft PowerPoint 2001. Modules were tested and are entirely compatible with Macintosh and Windows systems going back to PowerPoint 97. The modules may look slightly different depending on your system, monitor size, software version, installed fonts, or other factors. The "view" feature on your toolbar can be used to adjust the size of the slide image.

PRESENTATIONS AND SCRIPTS

The presentations range from 25 to 50 slides. Each presentation should run 60 to 75 minutes depending on the level of augmentation and audience participation. Questions from the participants can easily make a one-hour presentation stretch out to 90 minutes or more.

I suggest that you first read through the entire module in the book to give you a general "lay of the land." Here the speakers' scripts are reproduced along with the accompanying PowerPoint slides. The scripts are taken from notes and tapes of presentations I have given in the last year or so. My style for presenting technology-related concepts to groups is informal and rather conversational. This is reflected in the scripts.

Next customize the text as you see fit on the scripts offered on the CD-ROM. Note that the text presented in Roman type is the part of the script to say aloud. The italicized text enclosed in brackets < > are the stage directions supporting the script. Although you may want to use the presentations with only a few changes, I encourage you to experiment with customizing them for your own needs. Topics seem friendlier and allow participants in the class to create touchstones to their own lives. I discuss my hobbies, and relatives—even my dog. (My yellow Labrador Jake has been in so many of my talks that participants in my sessions have asked, "Is your dog in this one?") Always remember that it's fun to change these presentations to give them a personal, local flavor.

IMAGES AND SCREENSHOTS

All of the images in the PowerPoint presentations are from the Microsoft clipart galleries, screen shots from Web sites that graciously allowed me to include their content, and digital photos taken for this project or pulled from my personal archive of photos. All of the digital images, mostly found in the digital camera module, are stored in an images directory on the CD-ROM. Use them as needed as you manipulate the PowerPoint presentations.

The screenshots of Web sites found in the modules of the *Toolkit* are presented courtesy of their owners or creators. Permissions were obtained for all in preparation of publication of this work.

CAPTURING YOUR OWN SCREENSHOTS

New shots captured on your own PCs are easily inserted on the PowerPoint slides. If you insert your own screenshots, be sure to include URLs so participants can revisit the sites if they would like to.

On a Macintosh:
   Shift—Command—3 grabs the whole screen as a picture file.
   Shift—Command—4 grabs that section of the screen where the cursor resides as a picture file.

Place the picture file as you would like using PowerPoint's Insert feature.

On a PC:

With the desired window or Web site displayed, press the Print Screen key (to capture just the active window, press ALT + Print Screen). Open whatever program you want the image saved to (for example, Word or PowerPoint) and press Ctrl-V or go to Edit/Paste to place the document.

CREATING THE HANDOUTS

A separate directory on the CD-ROM contains handouts for each module in the form of PowerPoint documents. All Web sites discussed in the modules have the URLs listed on the PPT slide to facilitate easy creation of handouts. These are ready to be printed and photocopied for your class. Note that many times not every slide is needed in the handout packet, such as screenshots or large image slides like those found in the digital camera module. The handout files include only the pertinent slides. This saves paper and gives your audience only the useful information. Class packets can be created from the presentations by printing two, three, or six slides per page. People seem to appreciate three slides per page because PowerPoint automatically adds a few lines for notes next to each slide. For many of the presentations, I have found that the printed slides with some additional useful URLs are all that are needed. If you'd like to include all slides from the modules in a handout packet, simply print the module PowerPoint files themselves.

PROMOTING THE CLASSES

The CD-ROM includes a directory of simple fliers for each class. These are single PowerPoint slides that utilize graphics from the modules and a brief blurb about the class. Use them or create your own as needed to post around your library and on community bulletin boards.

In addition to the fliers, you can create a technologically savvy publicity machine for these classes. Promote them electronically on your library's Web site, other community Web sites, and by using a library program distribution list e-mailed weekly or monthly. Many Web sites offer free "mailing lists" or your library may have the needed software/hardware to have its own mailing list for programs. Gather e-mail addresses at classes and on survey forms or cards dropped off at service points. A "What's Happening at the Library" e-mail newsletter might be a welcome addition to your library's publicity functions. Check out Cleveland Public Library's "Net Notice" system for a look at this method in action: *www.cpl.org*.

PRESENTATION TIPS

Some basic presentation tips for all of the modules:

- Assemble and display the related materials—books, videos, and magazines relating to the topic—and make them available for checkout after the class.
- Determine the skill level of your group and present accordingly by slowing down or speeding up various portions of the module. Allow some flexibility with the material if you find a savvy audience eager for more detailed information. Be ready to go online if possible and demonstrate sample sites or concepts.
- Reiterate difficult points slowly if you feel some participants do not understand key concepts.

KEEPING THE *TOOLKIT* CURRENT

Throughout the text of the *The Library Internet Trainer's Toolkit*, you'll find hints to keep each module fresh in the introductions or in the text of the scripts. Here are some general helpers to keep each module up-to-date.

- Check the URLs in each module before printing handouts and before the class. Change them accordingly as Web site addresses change.
- Subscribe to mailing lists like NetTrain or Web4Lib to stay current with library technology and training news. For subscription instructions:
  Send e-mail to: *listserv@listserv.acsu.buffalo.edu* with no subject, and in the body (text) of the message include only this one line: subscribe NETTRAIN 'Firstname' 'Lastname' where 'Firstname' and 'Lastname' are replaced by your real name. Or send the message "subscribe Web4Lib your name" to *listserv@sunsite.berkeley.edu* (Web address: *http://sunsite.berkeley.edu/Web4Lib/*)
- Read professional periodicals with a technological slant like *Computers in Libraries* as well as the mainstream press: magazines like *Time, Newsweek,* and *Entertainment Weekly* often highlight what's new and hot on the technology or Internet landscape.
- Television programs like NBC's *Today* and specialized cable shows often highlight emerging or hot technology topics.
- Surf the Web to see what other libraries are doing with public Internet instruction.

What's the most important instruction to offer? Have fun with these topics! Enjoy *The Library Internet Trainer's Toolkit*—use it, change it, make it your own. Learning about computers and the Internet in a group setting is a great way to learn—and teach.

Acknowledgments

Special thanks to Charles Harmon, my editor, who helped this project grow from its beginnings over breakfast at Computers in Libraries 2000 conference until the final editing process in 2001. I appreciate his thoughtfulness, his suggestions, his confidence in me, and his patience during this process.

Thanks also to Michael Kelley and Kevin Allison at Neal Schuman for their help as we finished the project.

Thanks to my colleagues and coworkers at the St. Joseph County Public Library for their support: especially Linda Broyles, Coordinator of Networked Resources, Julie Hill, Valerie Simmons, David Heidt, Joyce Hug, and Adam Tarwacki, coolest circ clerk I know, who freely donated the use of his image and his experiences in chat.

Thanks to Dave Haslett, Head of the computer services staff of the St. Joseph County Public Library (SJCPL), and Harold Rowe, Joe Reimers and Sue Hostetler. Thanks to Sue for making that late night drive to my house to bring me a needed module on CD!

Thanks to Frances Walters, SJCPL Head of Children's Services, for her insight into children's safety on the Web and for reading over the finished script.

Thanks to the Administration of SJCPL for their encouragement and for giving me the opportunity to learn and explore so many emerging technologies.

A heartfelt thank you to George Barnum, Electronic Collection Manager at the Government Printing Office, who was always happy to read and critique raw pages of transcribed scripts, who assured me I was on the right track, who offered useful government Web sites, and who provided invaluable help with the index of this work. Thanks also for the use of his movie of the London nighttime bus ride.

Thanks to Cindy Etkin at the Government Printing Office who shared her excellent work on evaluating Web resources and allowed me to put up her pages at Tame the Web.

Thanks to Richard Truxall, Internet Trainer and Consultant, Jeff Humphrey at INCOLSA, and all of my other colleagues in the library training world who discussed this project with me. Thanks to the friendly people at all of the Web sites who allowed me to use screenshots.

Thanks to Becky Compise, eBay™ aficionado, for the use of her photos.

Personal thanks to my father, Lee Stephens, and my friends who were so supportive and understanding during the winter months of 2000/01 I spent writing: Steven Hoggatt, who walked Jake so many times, and Andrew McShane, for his help and unwavering humor.

Thanks to the people who allowed me to use their images in the Digital Camera module: Craig, Michelle, Dana, David, Valerie, and Jeremy.

Thanks to Carol Jewell, member of the Enchanted List for years, who helped me with a corrupt PowerPoint file.

Digital photographs and movies for the *Toolkit* were taken by Michael Stephens, Steven Hoggatt, or George Barnum.

Module 1
Introducing the
Personal Computer

INTRODUCTION

This module introduces library users to the basics of personal computers and many of the terms and acronyms associated with them. The presenter will define such terms as RAM, CPU, USB, and the like in easy-to-understand language for the beginner. This is the fundamental class that all the other modules build on.

I have presented this class over 40 times at the St. Joseph County Public Library (SJCPL); Mishawaka, Indiana, Public Library; and Bremen, Indiana, Public Library and each time it is different! The participants in the class, current computer news, and any number of influences can make presenting this module a new experience each time you present it. Questions may colour the class as well, from a discussion of children and computers to a lively Q & A about security and viruses.

With minor modifications, this presentation can also be called "So You Want to Buy a Computer?" and targeted at people getting ready to purchase. Additional handouts culled from computer buying guides in your library or a sampling of ads from the local paper augment this class. Be careful, however, not to advertise any type of computer or brand.

WORKSHOP ATTENDEES WILL GAIN:

1. A general understanding of personal computers, their hardware and software, as well as an overview of newer technologies.
2. Definitions of often-heard computer jargon and "techno-talk" in an easy-to-understand manner.
3. Hints and tips for getting started with personal computers.

TIPS FOR PRESENTING THIS MODULE

- Keep this module current:

    Check to see if the capacities of any large storage media have changed. The original version of this module discussed the SuperDisk by Imation but those disks have been discontinued.

    If new versions of operating systems are released, keep current by including their names: Macintosh OSX, Windows ME, etc.

    Watch the ads and other resources to gauge the speed of current processors. The 800MHz used in the module can be changed to 1–8 GHz or more as needed.

- If presenting in an auditorium or conference room, try to have a PC available for participants to examine and experiment with after the class. In a lab setting, allow participants to follow along by looking at their PCs—maybe moving the pointer with the mouse or actually launching the program. Determine the skill level of your group and present accordingly.

- Collect a few beginning computer books from your library and have them available in the presentation area for participants to peruse after the program.

- Have on hand a CD-ROM, floppy, Zip™, and Jaz™ disk—or as many as you can. Use them as visual aids when you discuss sizes and storage media.

- For the new technologies section, I have utilized my own digital camera to show participants what such devices can do. It's nice to actually have something to look at. Other devices, MP3 players, USB cables, homemade CDs, would be nice as well. Use what's available to you.

MODULE I—INTRODUCING THE PERSONAL COMPUTER—SCRIPT

Slide 1: Introduction

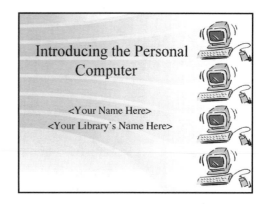

<Introduce yourself and your helper if you have one. Tell the group that you will be using a presentation program called PowerPoint to present the program.>

Slide 2: Our Plan

Local and national newspapers often advertise the latest deals from the big computer stores or department stores that sell computers. Or you might see ads for computers in magazines or other places. The ads are colourful, have a picture of a computer, and say "Computers are on sale—come and buy a computer!" This computer may have:

> 800 MHz processor
> 128 meg RAM
> 40 gig hard drive
> 40X CD-ROM drive
> 56k modem

What does all of that mean? It can be rather confusing, can't it? What we are here to do tonight is make sense of all of this! We'll define all of these things. Guess what—here's some homework: After class, look for one of these ads and see what you learned about all of these terms for practically any type of personal computer.

So, in this class we're going to discuss personal computers: basic applications, what programs you might use on your computer, and some of the new technologies that you are hearing about. Have you heard about "burning CDs" or "MP3"? Those are the things we'll discuss.

Our goal is to give you a basic understanding of a lot of the terminology we see in ads or in the media or hear people discuss when they talk about what kind of computer they have.

If you have a question or want a clarification, please don't hesitate to raise your hand or call out to me.

Slide 3: Personal Computers Defined

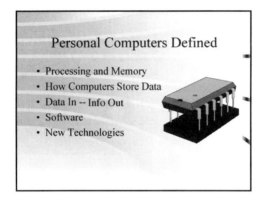

When we define personal computers, some of the things we talk about are: how the computer processes data, how it uses its memory, how it stores data, and what we get when we put information into the computer. We can also define our personal computer by describing what type of software or programs it has on it. And now we have to define many of the new technologies available to us today that make our PCs better and more fun.

Slide 4: Computer Diagram

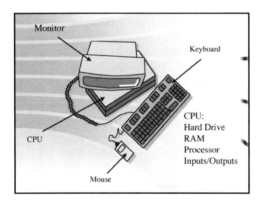

Here's our computer—a personal computer or PC—and all of its parts.

The **monitor** is your window into what goes on inside the computer. It allows you to see what you are typing when you are creating a letter or a report. It allows you to see the Internet when you connect and surf around. Connecting to the Internet and moving around is called surfing or browsing. The monitor is like a TV set in many ways.

The **keyboard** is just like a typewriter keyboard but a little more fancy. It allows you to input or key in words. Just like the typewriter we learned to type on, all of the letters are there with a few extra keys as well. Across the top of the keyboard are keys with Fs on them. Those are called **function keys** and they make various things happen in programs. On the right-hand side of the keyboard is a set of numbers like calculator or adding machine numbers. These are excellent for inputting numeric data.

Attached to the computer or keyboard is the **mouse**. The mouse moves the pointer on the screen. We also call the pointer the cursor in some applications. Xerox was one of the companies that introduced the mouse in the late 1970s and Apple Computer put a mouse on its first Macintosh in 1984. The mouse allows us to select and deselect items on the screen. You select items by clicking on them. Note that most mice have two buttons—a right and a left button, and each of them performs different functions.

Slide 5: CPU Diagram

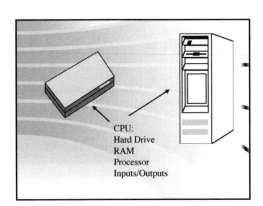

Finally, the most important part of the computer setup is the **CPU**. That stands for **Central Processing Unit**. The CPU is the brain of the computer.

Our slide has two types of CPUs—a desktop model and a tower model. The CPU on the left is the desktop model, also called a "pizza box" by some people. The "pizza box" sits beneath your monitor on a desk. On the right is the tower model. It's usually tall and sits next to your desk on the floor or on a computer table.

The CPU—Central Processing Unit—has all of the items listed inside of it and we're going to define each of them: hard drive, RAM, processor, and inputs and outputs. The inputs/outputs are where we plug stuff into the CPU—like a printer or phone line.

Slide 6: Processing, Memory, Storage, and Connection

Back to our numbers we mentioned at the start.
    800 MHz processor
    128 meg RAM
    40 gig hard drive
    40X CD-ROM drive
    56k modem
So let's take these one by one and discuss them.

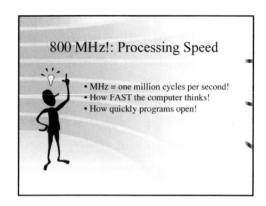

Slide 7: 800 MHz!: Processing Speed

The 800 MHz processor.

That is the **speed of your processor,** which is the brain of your computer. Megahertz is one million cycles per second or one million computations per second. To put it another way, a little simpler, it means that your computer thinks 800 million times per second to do what it does for you: How quickly your programs open and your documents are saved and changed depends on how fast the processor works.

It might be 800, it might be a higher or lower number. Remember those computers that were called a 286 or 386? That refers to the speed of the processor. Now we're running at much faster speeds.

We can also describe the processor by calling it by the manufacturer's name: Intel or Pentium. Have you seen commercials or ads for these companies? So when we talk about processors, the numbers mean how fast it thinks, how fast the computer does its job.

Questions?

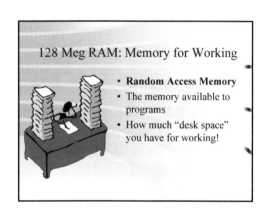

Slide 8: 128 Meg RAM: Memory for Working

RAM is Random Access Memory. It is the memory for working in your computer. It is how much space you have. Picture your desktop. You have a certain amount of space on that desk to work. You might be writing a letter or painting a picture. You might want to have one more thing going and run out of space! That's what RAM is—your space for working.

RAM is also temporary. Whatever is there disappears when you turn off your computer. It's not where you save stuff you're working on, but where it sits while you work on it.

Think of it, again, as your desk space where you open your programs.

Questions?

Slide 9: 40 Gig Hard Drive: Memory for Storage

The **hard drive** is our memory for storage. RAM is where we work—the desktop—but the hard drive is where we store all the stuff we work on and work with. It is built in to your computer. It has storage for your programs and your documents. I like to think of it as a huge filing cabinet sitting next to my desk where I can store what I'm working on. You can have a certain amount of stuff on your desktop, but you can have a lot more stuff stored in your filing cabinet.

Questions?

Slide 10: 40X CD-ROM Drive

<Hold up a CD-Rom disc>

Here's a **CD-ROM** disc. It looks just like a music CD, but it's made for a CD-ROM drive. CD-ROM stands for **Compact Disc Read Only Memory**. That means that the information on the disc is set in stone. Once it is made it is a read-only disc. You cannot write or save something else to a CD-ROM. In a few minutes, we'll discuss **CDR**, but for now please remember that a CD-ROM can't be changed.

The CD-ROM drive reads the information off of the disc with a laser. We'll define CD-ROM a bit more in a moment, but what we need to understand here is that the 40X is the speed that the data is pulled off the CD.

Way back when the first CD-ROMs were developed, they spun at a certain speed for pulling off the data. Later, of course, developers found a way to make the discs spin about twice as fast as the first ones. That was called the 2X CD-ROM drive. So, what do you think 40X is?

<Allow audience to answer.>

Right—it spins 40 times as fast as the first one. That's very fast!

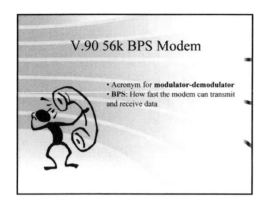

Slide 11: V. 90 56k BPS Modem

We'll also get a **modem** with our computer. Modem is an acronym for **modulator-demodulator**. That's a really techie term to describe the device that connects your computer to a phone line and lets it communicate with other computers. If we have an account with an Internet Service Provider, we use the modem to dial out and connect to it. We might also dial out to a computer line going into our library or local college to look for books, and so on.

The term **BPS** stands for bits per second—that's how fast the modem can transmit and receive data. We'll talk about bits and bytes and kilobytes in just a second.

Slide 12: How Computers Store Data

First, let's talk about how computers store data. Data for our purposes might be any documents we create or the programs we use to create them. We store data by "writing" the information onto a disk that the computer can come back to and read later.

We'll use our hard drive to store data—especially all of the software that comes with our machine. We might also use disks that are inserted into a disk drive. We might use floppy disks, CD-ROM, and newer high-capacity storage disks like Zip™, or Jaz™.

<Here I usually make a comment about how the computer industry loves snazzy names!>

Slide 13: How Computers Store Data

We store data on different disks, but for it all to make sense we need to discuss what all this talk is about bytes and megs and gigs. That's how we talk about the size of the data we store on a disk.

A byte is a single character of text. It is composed of 8 bits—the smallest unit of measurement in our computer jargon. One thousand bytes, roughly, is a kilobyte. A letter to my aunt in Seattle typed on my computer might be 12k. That's reasonably small. A digital picture of my dog Jake, however, might be 345k.

<Hold up a 3.5 inch floppy.>

Here's a standard **floppy disk**. Why is it called a floppy when it has this hard case? It's because inside the hard case is a thin magnetic disk that's very floppy. Anyway, a disk like this could hold a lot of letters to my aunt but maybe just three or four pictures of Jake.

One thousand kilobytes is a megabyte. Remember the **meg** we discussed earlier when we talked about RAM, random access memory? That's what we are talking about—a thousand kilobytes make a meg. 128 meg of RAM is 128,000k of RAM!

One thousand megabytes is a gigabyte. That's how we talk about hard drive space. Remember our 40 gig hard drive? That's 40,000 meg. Or a great deal of storage space!

Let's review: One thousand bytes make up one kilobyte. One thousand kilobytes become a megabyte—we use megs when we talk about our RAM. One thousand meg is a gigabyte—and 40, 50, or 60 gig is usually the size of our hard drive.

Slide 14: Floppies and CD-ROMs

<Hold up floppy disk again.>
Remember this—the floppy disk? This disk holds 1.44 megabytes of data—a whole lot of letters or a handful of pictures.

<Hold up a CD-ROM.>

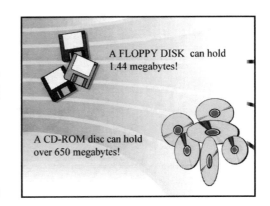

A FLOPPY DISK can hold 1.44 megabytes!

A CD-ROM disc can hold over 650 megabytes!

The **CD-ROM** holds anywhere from 650 to 700 megabytes of data, but as we discussed earlier, it's set in stone. Once it is created you cannot change a CD-ROM. What might we find on CD-ROM? We'll find games, lots of games, and children's educational programs as well as encyclopedias filled with loads and loads of data! Remember—up to 700 meg of stuff.

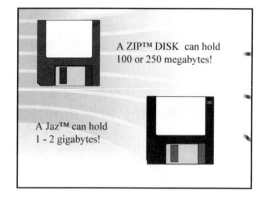

Slide 15: Zip™ and Jaz™ Disks

<Hold up a Zip™ disk if you have them at your library. If the storage capacity has changed, update these numbers.>

A **Zip™ disk** is one of the newer high-capacity storage disks. Notice it's bigger and a little thicker than the floppy. You need a special drive—a Zip™ drive—to read and write to these disks. But these disks hold 100 or 250 meg of data. That's a lot for storing your writing or pictures.

If you are out looking at computers or looking at the ads, you might see systems that come with built-in Zip™ disk drives or the Zip™'s big brother—the Jaz™ drive. A **Jaz™ disk** can hold 1000 meg—remember what a thousand megs is?—a gigabyte. Jaz disks can even hold 2 gigabytes. So you might have the option to get a computer with one of these drives, or you might be at a computer store where they put together a system for you. You may want to include one of these high-capacity storage disks.

Questions?

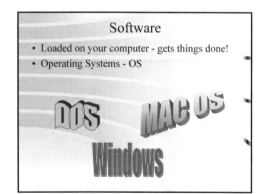

Slide 16: Software

Now, we've discussed at length the hardware involved in our computers, let's talk about software. Software is loaded on your computer's hard drive and it helps you get things done.

The most important software on your computer is the **operating system**—the software that is always there, is always on, and makes your computer do its job. DOS was an early operating system. DOS stands for Disk Operating System and it is still the basis for Windows. The Macintosh system is simply known as the Mac OS. Most of you are familiar with Windows. What Windows is, be it Windows 95 or the new Windows 2000, is an operating system.

Slide 17: The GUI: Graphical User Interface

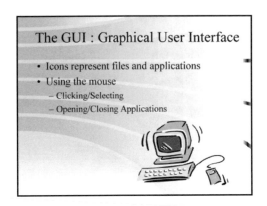

Windows and the Mac OS are also known as GUIs. The GUI (**Graphical User Interface**) allows us to see our applications or programs as well as our documents and data. The GUI uses icons—little pictures—to represent different parts of your computer. In Windows we might see in the top left corner of the screen a little computer that's labelled "My Computer." If we click on that, it opens a window that displays the contents of your hard drive. That's how a Graphical User Interface works.

It allows you to see your files, to open and close programs, and to print your documents. Using the mouse to point and click is part of the GUI. Keyboarding is also part of the GUI.

Using a mouse may be difficult for you at first if you have never done it before. It just takes practice.

Slide 18: Basic Applications

What else then, speaking of word processing programs, will we find on our computer. If you buy a PC these days, you probably will get something called bundled software with it, meaning a set of software programs that come preloaded on your machine.

One thing every computer will probably have is a **word processing program**. Word processing allows us to create really nice looking letters, reports, or other printed material with our computers and then print them out. We'll look at an example in just a second.

Database programs allow us to organize information in an orderly fashion.

<Use your own database example here.>

For example, I keep a database of my CD collection. In a database you create different fields of data for each item in the list. I have fields for artist, album title, year it was recorded, and so forth. The database program then allows me to sort the CDs by artist or group, by year, and other fields.

Here's another example of databases at work: All of

the materials in our library are catalogued in a database that includes fields about author, title, year of publication, and so on. And—how many of you have a library card? All of you who have cards are in a database of library users. The fields for each of you might include items such as your address or phone number. When you borrow a book, the two databases meet and match that title to your record. That's how we know what you have borrowed.

Spreadsheet software allows us to keep track of numerical data, rather like a database but more powerful, with numbers and formulas. I'll show you an example in a moment.

Graphics programs allow us to manipulate images. To change them, or clean them up, or have fun with them. Have you seen the commercial where a man uses his computer to paste his face on a muscular body? That's a graphics program doing its job.

Finally, all of these things have one similar feature. Most programs or applications or software have a **common interface**. That means that the tools and options look the same across each different program. Microsoft programs are an example of how this works. Let's look at some pictures of programs and I'll show you what I mean.

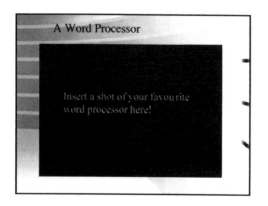

Slide 19: Word Processor

<Tailor this text for the shot of the program you use. Include on the screen some text formatted with a fancy font to show off the capabilities of the program.>

Here's a sample **word processing** program. In word processing I can type in words then change them: make them bigger, change their style and colour, and do some really creative things. But look at the interface as well. That's the menu options up at the top, like File, Edit, Insert.

Here's the **spreadsheet**.

Slide 20: Spreadsheet

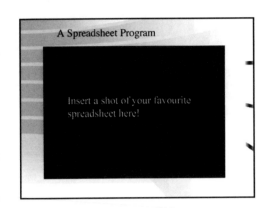

<Insert a spreadsheet shot here, maybe a spreadsheet you use in your job that includes formulas and numbers. Explain what your example does: formulas, sums, and so on.>

Notice that the spreadsheet includes many of the same options: File, Edit, and so forth.

This means that, once you learn one program, it's easier to learn the second because you already know a lot about how it works.

Slide 21: Image Editing Software

<You may want to just say "a dog.">

Here's my dog Jake that has been brought into a **graphics program** and changed into a watercolour print by just selecting some options. It's very easy to do and looks really great. He's also been changed into a mosaic tile design and a neon glow.

In fact, many of the flashy ads we see in magazines were probably created with pictures and a graphics manipulation program. And movies like *Titanic, Jurassic Park*, and *<insert new special-effects movie here>* are enhanced with a souped-up version of graphics programs called CGI programs: **Computer Generated Images**.

Slide 22: Other Equipment

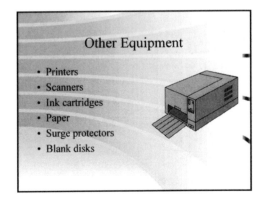

Here are some other items that might come bundled with your new computer. Any external device attached to a computer is called a **peripheral**. Examples of peripherals include printers, disk drives, newer technologies like CD burners, and even monitors, keyboards, and mice.

A **printer**. Most probably your new printer will be an ink jet printer. That type of printer uses ink cartridges to squirt the ink on paper very precisely and usually in colour or black. Cartridges last awhile, unless you are printing lots of full-colour pages. Today's printers are very high quality. Bear in mind that while lower-end printers are getting better and better, the more you pay, the more features the printer will have. The key to look for is the number of **dots per inch** or **DPI**—the higher the DPI, the better the print quality. You can even feed photo-grade paper though them and print out nice looking photos.

A **scanner**. This device allows you to pull an image into your computer like photocopying. You place the photo face down on glass, close the lid, and start scanning with software. Then you see your image on the screen and you can pull it into graphics programs or use it in documents.

What might we do with a scanner? Here's a favourite example of mine. You have at home a box of all the family photos going back years and years. You could scan all of them into your computer to save, to print, and to archive. Remember this example because we will come back to it.

Other items that probably will come with your computer or that you may want to pick up are extra ink cartridges, paper for your printer, surge protectors to plug everything into to keep it safe from spikes in your electricity, and blank disks to store or back up your work.

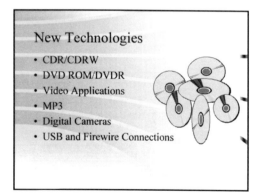

Slide 23: New Technologies

To conclude our programme, I want to tell you about some of the new technologies you may be hearing about these days—new hardware and devices that can enhance your computer and your use of it. Some of these you may have heard of. Some may be new to you.

First up is CDR. CDR stands for **Compact Disc Recordable**. A CDR drive has the capability to record data to a CD-ROM. So, you can write 650 to 700 megs of data on a CDR. Once it's written it's set in stone like the CD-ROMs mentioned earlier.

What can we save onto CDR? All of our documents for the year. All of your letters or creations. Remember those scans of all the family photos? You could record all of those on CDR and then go to the family Christmas dinner and give a copy to everyone: "Here's the family photos on CD."

The young person in your life comes into the room and says, "I just burned a CD of my favourite songs." What does that mean? That means that you can also create regular music CDs with a CDR drive. To burn a CD means to record a CD. You might also hear these drives called CD burners. It is worth noting that it is in fact illegal under copyright law in the UK to burn a CD of songs copied from another source without permission, although it is not generally enforced as long as the copy made is for private use. However, if the burned CD were copied on and sold this would be piracy and would definitely be enforced.

We said that a CDR is permanent once it's burned or recorded. Most CDR drives are also CDRW compatible, meaning they are **CD rewritable**. You can record a bit of data and then come back to it later and record more. You can erase and rewrite the CDRW many times.

CDRs can cost about 50 pence each. CDRWs will cost a bit more because you can reuse them.

DVD ROM is a new thing as well. You know that movies are coming out in a new format called DVD. DVD stands for **Digital Versatile Disk**. (We even circulate them out of our library.) You can play DVD movies on your computer with a DVD drive. Many DVDs include DVD ROM content: data that can be read by a special DVD drive in your computer. It might be background on the movie, games, or the like. DVD ROMs will work only in DVD ROM drives, not CD-ROM drives.

DVD RAM is recordable DVD and it is incredibly expensive. However, in a few years it will become commonplace, just like CD-ROMs before it.

Both the CDR and DVD drives are options you can add to your computer, or if you are buying a new system, you might choose one with a built-in CDR or DVD.

Video is making a big splash in the computing world, allowing people to edit their home videos on their computers with **digital video editing software**. Have you seen the Apple iMac commercials where the kids are jumping on the bed and the text says "Movie by Dad"? That's an example of making a movie on a computer. You use special software that pulls video into your hard drive. You can edit it, add titles and features like dissolves and fades. Then you can output or "print" the video to your VCR. Know this: Video takes up megs and megs of space, so you'll need a huge hard drive if this is something you are interested in.

MP3 is making a lot of news lately. It's simply a file type for music that can be easily exchanged over the Internet. A CD-quality, four-minute song might use 40 meg of space on your computer, but as an MP3 file it is compacted down to 4 meg without losing any quality. That's an easy size to exchange. MP3 causes controversy because it's very easy to turn any song off a CD into an MP3 and send it to someone online. That violates copyright laws and that's what all the hubbub has been about.

There are new little devices called MP3 players that can store songs from your personal collection. They work just like a portable CD player, but they're much smaller and hold more music.

Digital Cameras are next. How many of you have a digital camera or know someone who does?

<Allow audience to respond.>

Digital cameras are a new type of camera that takes pictures on disks instead of film. Remember our floppies? They are made of magnetic media. A digital camera grabs an image just like a regular camera, but instead of exposing the image on film writes it to magnetic media like a floppy or a high-capacity disk. Many cameras have little disks about the size of a matchbook that might hold 32 or 64 megs of images.

What can you do with a digital camera? Everything you do with a film camera and more, because you are not worrying about film and developing. Instead, you just need storage space and your computer to view the pictures. With the Internet, it's easy to e-mail a photo to someone else. A new dad brings his digital camera to the hospital and snaps mother and baby. Then, in a few minutes he's sending that picture to friends and relatives all over the world.

Finally, **USB connections** and **Firewire** are new ways of hooking devices up to your computer. If you are buying a new computer these days, you probably will get one with USB—that's **Universal Serial Bus** in techie talk—and maybe Firewire. Both offer a quick and easy way to add on to your computer. It might be an extra hard drive, a scanner, a CD burner, or a digital camera. Both of these ways of connecting devices to your computer are very fast, especially Firewire. It's great for digital video and the like.

Remember the ads we talked about at the beginning of the program? Here's a bit more for your homework. Look at the ads for all the extra devices we've discussed that use USB or Firewire.

Slide 24: Thanks!

Well, we have covered a lot of material in our time together. How do you all feel? Are there any questions?

Please take a look at the books about computers we have here and the Web sites we have listed on the handouts.

Thanks!

Module 2
Navigating the
Internet and the
World Wide Web

INTRODUCTION

This module introduces library users to the basics of the Internet and the World Wide Web (WWW) and prepares them to become seasoned Web surfers. The presenter will describe what the Internet is, where it came from, and how participants can get access. If you would like a general introduction to the subject, I recommend NetLearn, an award-winning directory of resources for learning about the Internet. NetLearn provides resources for Web based materials, e-mail resources, downloadable programs, non-computer based materials, teaching resources, special resources and other directories of resources. NetLearn is hosted by The Robert Gordon University at *www.rgu.ac.uk/schools/sim/research/netlearn/callist.htm.*

This class has been around a long time. Versions of it have been presented at the St. Joseph County Public Library (SJCPL) since 1995! Currently, it's a requirement that virtually all of the reference staff at SJCPL be able to present this class.

WORKSHOP ATTENDEES WILL GAIN:

1. An understanding of the basic framework and history of the Internet.
2. An examination of the three main functions of the Internet.
3. A detailed understanding of the World Wide Web.

TIPS FOR PRESENTING THIS MODULE

- If possible, have a live Internet connection in your presentation room and take the participants online briefly after the talk to reinforce some of your points. A quick visit to a WWW subject list like the BUBL Link 5:15 (*www.bubl.ac.uk/link/*) or the Open Directory Project (*www.dmoz.org*) to show links and illustrate "surfing" is a nice note on which to end the session. Or you might direct them to the public Internet terminals in your library and allow them a few minutes of surfing with you and a helper standing by to assist.
- Collect a few beginning Internet books from your library and have them available in the presentation area for participants to peruse or check out after the programme.

MODULE 2—NAVIGATING THE INTERNET AND THE WORLD WIDE WEB—SCRIPT

Slide 1: Introduction

<Introduce yourself and your helper if you have one. Tell the group that you will be using a presentation program called PowerPoint to present the programme.>

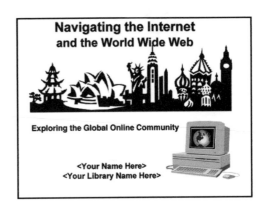

Navigating the Internet
and the World Wide Web

Exploring the Global Online Community

<Your Name Here>
<Your Library Name Here>

Slide 2: Our Goal

Here is our plan for this class: We will explore what the Internet is, briefly see where it came from, and learn how you can get on the Internet and what you can find there. I will introduce and define some of the terms and jargon you might hear when people talk about the Internet and about the World Wide Web.

Our goal is to answer these questions:

■What is the Internet?
■Where did it come from?
■How can you get on the Internet?
■What will you find there?

Slide 3: What in the world is the Internet?

What is the Internet then? It is a big network made up of little networks. Networks are groups of computers hooked together that can exchange information. This library <or substitute school or university> has a network of computers. <Local college> has many networks of computers for students and teachers. Businesses have networks. The Internet is a network of networks—meaning it's all of these networks in town, in the UK, and in the world connected together. It is the largest, most complex network in the world!

What in the world is the Internet?

The Internet is the largest group of
computers ever linked together.
(network of networks)

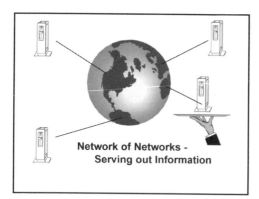

Slide 4: Network of Networks

These networks contain special computers that store information and serve it out as needed to those who connect to them. "Serve" is a good word because you might have heard of **servers**—that's another name for computers that store information and direct it out to people when they request it. So this network of networks is made up of lots of computers or servers, all over the world, that hold information and—

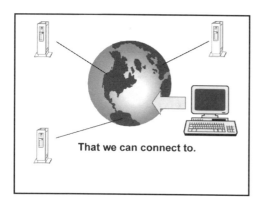

Slide 5: We Can Connect to These Networks.

—we have access to that information. We connect to these servers and can read about virtually any topic.

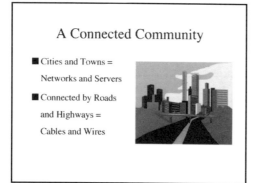

Slide 6: A Connected Community

Here's one of my favorite ways to think about the Internet: It's a connected community of servers and networks. Like cities and towns, these virtual "places" are linked together by wires and cables just like roads and highways. You've heard the phrase "Information Superhighway"—that's a great way to think of it.

Again, this community is global. It includes servers all over the world, from the UK to Australia, from the USA to Russia; in fact, everywhere.

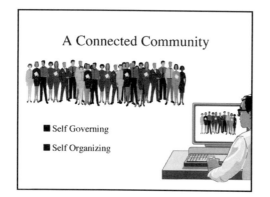

Slide 7: A Connected Community

It is also important to know that it is a connected community of *people*. The Internet is a community that you participate in. There is something for everyone on the Internet—for any interest, hobby, fascination, or curiosity that you have, you'll probably find a community on the Internet that deals with it.

Because the Internet is a community made up of many people with diverse backgrounds and interests, we might hear about stuff on the Internet that does not interest us specifically or that we might not want to see or know about. Or we might not want the young people in our lives to have access to certain information. Please realize, however, that adult oriented sites are just one small fraction of the wealth of information found on the Internet.

I should say at this point that the Internet is also self-organizing and self-governing. There is no one entity or group or organization that heads the Internet. There is no one place you can contact, no 0800 number you can call to complain about the Internet or ask for assistance. Each of those virtual cities and towns takes care of itself.

Slide 8: How long has the Internet been around?

How long has the Internet been around? You'll be surprised to know that it's been here longer than we think. Not since the time of the dinosaurs but since the early 1960s!

Slide 9: Internet History 101

Here's a one-minute Internet history lesson. In the early 1960s the government and the scientific community of the USA got together to develop a computer network that could exchange information between sites all over the USA. This was called the **Advanced Research Projects Administration Network** or **ARPANET**. It was created by the military for use in extreme circumstances—the USA was still in the grip of the Cold War.

This early network could exchange messages between computers via cabling that had nothing to do with the phone lines. So if something happened to phone lines in Denver, a message could still get from New York to Los Angeles with this network.

Here was the basis for e-mail!

The US government kept ARPANET to itself for a

long time but finally let the technology that created it roll down to the educational and scientific communities—where the **National Science Foundation** developed **NSFNET**. This allowed universities throughout the world to exchange information on research and scholarly topics.

With major capacity and speed improvements, in the late 1980s the Internet was born. Since then, computers have become more prevalent and more affordable. **The Graphical User Interface**—the Macintosh and Windows systems—allowed the creation of the World Wide Web.

The Internet has exploded in the last few years as an incredibly popular means of linking the world together and offering access to information easily and at a low cost.

Network of Computer Networks

■ **These networks all communicate using common protocols (rules): TCP/IP.**

■ **This allows the computers to talk to each other.**

Slide 10: Network of Computer Networks

Let me tell you a bit more about the network of networks. This network is made up of computers all over the world that communicate or exchange information with each other. To do this they use a common set of rules or protocols. These protocols allow us to connect to a server and access information on it. They allow us to have an e-mail account and send and receive messages from our friends and relatives. They allow us to exchange files with other users.

These rules are called **TCP/IP rules**. That stands for Transmission Control Protocol/Internet Protocol. Do not worry about this techie stuff too much but know that these rules—these protocols—allow us to "surf the net."

Network of Computer Networks

■ **EVERY computer on the Internet has its own unique numerical address.**

■ **IP Address: 206.64.228.12**

■ **IP numbers translate to words.**

Slide 11: Network of Computer Networks

Every computer on the Internet has its own unique numerical address. Following the rules I just told you about, it is called an **IP address**. An Internet Protocol address is made up of a string of numbers that identify that computer on the huge global network.

Here's a sample IP address: 206.64.228.12. That might be the address for some computer somewhere on the Internet.

Wouldn't you hate to have to remember a long stream of numbers for every Internet site you would like to go to?—Because we are human and it's easier to remember words instead of numbers, some of our IP rules translate that string of numbers into words. For example, that IP number might actually be the numerical equivalent of *www.<notable company here>.com*. That's an address you are probably familiar with!

Slide 12: Addressing on the Net

There really are two types of addresses on the Internet: Web addresses and e-mail addresses. Let's talk about these Web addresses now that you know they originally start out as strings of numbers.

Web addresses are everywhere, aren't they? Have you noticed them these days in the newspaper, in magazines, on television? Where have you seen a Web address lately?

<Allow audience to respond.>

Does anyone have a favorite Web address—a favorite site to surf to?

<Allow audience to respond.>

Great! Here are some of my favorite addresses. You can learn a lot about a Web address by looking at the different parts of the address. Here's another name for Web address, which seems techie but is useful to know: **URL**. URL stands for **Uniform Resource Locator**. That's a fancy way to say "Web address." Someone might ask you, "What's the URL of your Web page?" They are really asking for the address.

Here are some of my favourite URLs.

<Feel free to insert on this slide your favorite URLs but try to include .com, .ac (maybe the local college or university), and .org. Finish the list with your own library's URL.>

We can learn a lot about addresses like these. For

Addressing on the Net

■ Web Addresses
  (Uniform Resource Locators)
  – http:// www.amazon.com
  – http:// www.centerforhistory.org
  – http:// www.nd.edu
  – http://www.<your library URL>
■ E-mail
  – president@whitehouse.gov
  – <your e-mail here>

example, "the http://" will always be there and that stands for **Hypertext Transfer Protocol**. The "www" probably will be there, but not always. Following it will be the identifying name of the server—Amazon or Microsoft or whatever. Ideally, that tells you what the entity is that runs the site or what information you will find there.

Most telling is the last part of the address. Some call it an extension; some call it a zone. The .com or .org or .ac tells us what type of an organization it is. Can someone tell us what a .com is?

<Allow audience to respond.>

A .com is a business or commercial entity. Commercial—that's where the .com comes from. We see a lot of these around. In fact, it's now common to use the words "dot-com" to discuss Internet or World Wide Web businesses.

How about .co.uk? It's very similar to .com, in that it identifies the site as a commercial site based in the UK. However, because .com is seen as 'the' address to have, many UK companies have chosen a .com address instead of, or in addition to a .co.uk address.

What do you think about .org?

<Allow audience to respond.>

Yes. An organization. More specifically, a nonprofit organization like the historical society listed here or any other not-for-profit group.

What about .ac?

<Allow audience to respond.>

Yes. The .ac signifies a university or college—"academic".

What other extensions can you think of?

<Allow audience to respond.>

<Hopefully, you'll touch on .gov as government, .net as Internet-related (or used if the .com has already been

*used), possibly .mil for military, and so forth. Be ready
with examples of each to reinforce:*
  www.ukonline.gov.uk *(UK Government information
  services)*
  www.inlandrevenue.gov.uk *(UK Inland Revenue department)*
  www.<local ISP?>.net *(e.g. www.demon.net)*
*Use as many local examples as possible to bring these
ideas "home".>*

All of these .com and .ac and .org addresses are also
known as **Domain Names**. A domain name is the name
of the main server that hosts or serves a business's or
organization's pages. The domain *www.tesco.com* im-
plies that information about the supermarket is there.
The server is their "realm" on the Web . . . their *domain*. We'll talk a bit more about domains in just a
few minutes.

*<For this next section, I'll use the St. Joseph County
Public Library URL. Feel free to substitute your own
or that of a nearby library if you do not have a Web
presence yet.>*

Then here is a URL for our library! Take a look:
http://www.sjcpl.lib.in.us. We know what the *http*
means and we know what *www* stands for. Look at
the rest: *sjcpl* is St. Joseph County Public Library in
Indiana in the United States.

That's another type of extension: the country code.
US for United States, and so on. What do you think
DE is?

<Allow audience to respond.>

AU?

<Allow audience to respond.>

JP?

<Allow audience to respond.>

Okay, the second type of address is an e-mail address. How many of you already have an e-mail address?

<Allow audience to respond.>

An e-mail address is made up of two parts, separated by the @ (at) symbol. The first represents you: your name, initials, or nickname, based on how the mail provider chooses to create addresses. Sometimes, providers allow you to choose a name. It might be a nickname or reflect something you like or collect. If Jane Smith loves to collect Beanie Babies, she might be beaniejane. After the @ symbol is the name of the computer or server that handles your mail.

For those of you with e-mail addresses: Think about what your address is? What server do you use? Would anyone like to share the name of his or her mail server?

<Allow audience to respond.>

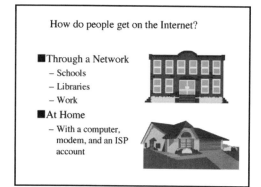

How do people get on the Internet?

■Through a Network
  – Schools
  – Libraries
  – Work
■At Home
  – With a computer,
    modem, and an ISP
    account

Slide 13: How do people get on the Internet?

So, we understand where the Internet came from, how it works, and how addresses work on the Net. The next thing we'll discuss is how we can get on the Net. There are two ways we can do that. One way is through a network at school, at a library like this one, or at work. Who has Internet access at work?

<Allow audience to respond.>

Here's a fun term for what some people do at work when they're looking at Internet stuff on company time—cyberslacking. There are studies being done now about access at work and how much time people spend surfing.

Let's get back to schools and libraries. Isn't it wonderful how many schools are becoming wired and have access to the Internet through their own networks? Likewise the library world has changed drastically since the Internet and the World Wide Web exploded on the scene in the early 1990s.

The other way we might get access to the Internet is through a home connection with a computer, a modem, and an account with an **Internet Service Provider**. A **modem** is a **modulator-demodulator** device that allows us to dial out and connect to an Internet provider. When you use a modem on your phone line, your phone will be busy if you are connected to the Internet.

Slide 14: Internet Service Providers

Internet Service Providers will offer you an account that gives you access to the World Wide Web. You'll get an account name, a password, and usually an e-mail address. You'll also get the software you need to put on your computer to get your modem to make the connection.

Many providers began first as national online services that offered their own content—access to news, hobbies, popular culture, and more, as well as discussion areas. When the Internet became big, the larger providers like **America Online** and **CompuServe** had to realign and make connections to the Internet available as well. A lot of national companies want to be your Internet provider.

There are also a lot of local companies that offer the same services and the same connection. Take a look at the phone book under Internet Providers to see a list of local companies that provide Internet access.

> ### Internet Service Providers
>
> ■ Companies sell a connection to the Internet.
> ■ Some began as national online services, like AOL or Compuserve.
> ■ Many are local businesses.

Slide 15: Choosing an ISP

To help you make your decision, here is a list of things to remember when choosing an Internet Service Provider. It's always good to talk to friends and relatives and see what provider they recommend.

First, what is the ISP's orientation? Is it for business accounts or personal accounts or both? You might need a business account if you want to establish a presence for your business on the Internet. Personal accounts are what we have been discussing: accounts for the home user. Most providers, especially local ones, will offer both types of services.

Second, what type of performance and availability

> ### Choosing an ISP
>
> ■ Orientation - Business/Personal
> ■ Performance and Availability - Busy Signals?
> ■ Speed and Types of Connection - Modem, Cable, DSL?

do they offer? Here you might have to talk to people you know and ask them about a certain provider. Do they get busy signals? That might mean the ISP has too many users and not enough incoming lines. At 8 p.m. on a weeknight, we've had dinner, relaxed, maybe walked the dog or played with the kids, and we want to check our e-mail. Is the line busy? That can be frustrating.

What speed and types of connection do the ISPs offer? Strictly modem connections or also some of the newer types of connections: cable modems and ADSL?

Cable modems are devices that connect your computer to the Internet through the cable lines you might have already coming into your home for your television. Cable modems offer increased speed and an "always-on" connection.

ADSL stands for **Asymmetric Digital Subscriber Line** and it is one of the newest and fastest ways to connect to the Internet. It allows users to stay connected all the time instead of having to dial in and tie up the phone line. DSL costs a bit more than regular ISP phone line connections, but many serious Internet users find its increased speed and ease of use enticing.

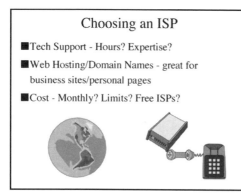

Choosing an ISP

■ Tech Support - Hours? Expertise?

■ Web Hosting/Domain Names - great for business sites/personal pages

■ Cost - Monthly? Limits? Free ISPs?

Slide 16: Choosing an ISP

When choosing an ISP we need to consider what type of technical support they provide. What are their hours of service? Is the support automated or do you talk or e-mail with a human?

Say it's 8 p.m. on a Wednesday night and you want to check your e-mail or surf the Web and you can't connect. Is there someone at your ISP who can help you? Does she have the expertise or do you get, "Well, I don't know about your problem but I'll leave a message for so-and-so who's here in the daytime . . . ."

Remember there is nothing wrong with calling an ISP and asking the people who work there about their hours. Some ISPs even advertise that they have 24-hour customer support.

Other services to consider: Web hosting and domain names. You might want a personal Web page eventually or you may want one for your business endeavors.

Remember we discussed the domain name as the main server or site for a business or organization? You can actually buy a domain name and then find an ISP to "host" it for you. That means that the ISP will store the files on one of their servers. That's great for business sites or personal pages. Remember Jane? She may buy *www.janesbeanies.com* to highlight her collection or to sell or trade Beanies. How much does a domain cost? Anything from a few pounds to several hundred, depending on which facilities you require.

Naturally, cost is a factor for getting an account with an ISP. How much will the ISP charge you for access? Will it be monthly? Are you committed for a set period? What limits might they have? Some ISPs have no time limits while others may limit users to 90 hours or so a month. Shop around and find a plan that's best for you!

We should also mention the newer free ISPs. These services offer a free connection to the Internet with e-mail for no cost. The only catch is that while you are surfing the ISP displays a window or box on your screen that has advertisements in it that constantly change. It's like watching television shows and commercials at the same time.

Any questions?

<This is a good place to officially ask for questions, although I do it more often depending on the group. There is often confusion about ISPs, domains, monthly fees, and so on.>

Slide 17: Functions of the Internet

So now we have our understanding of the Internet, we've found a good Internet provider, and we are ready to dive in. What will we find on the Internet? The Internet has three main functions or uses: messaging, remote login, and file transfer.

Let's look at each of these and discuss them.

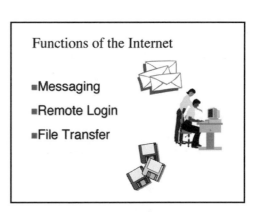

Functions of the Internet

- Messaging
- Remote Login
- File Transfer

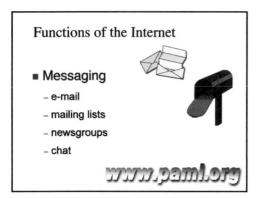

Slide 18: Functions of the Internet—Messaging

Messaging is probably the most popular use of the Internet. E-mail is one form and we've discussed what an e-mail address is. But what is e-mail exactly? It's an **electronic message** that travels from one Internet user to another. E-mail allows me to send a message to my <cousin in Washington state> or my <friend who works in Washington, D.C.>.

Other types of messaging on the Internet include participating in e-mail discussion lists, newsgroups, and chatting.

Let's talk about each of these. An e-mail discussion list is a means of exchanging information or discussing a particular topic with others via your e-mail account. <For example, I might belong to the Labrador retriever mailing list because I have a big yellow Lab named Jake!>

A mailing list is hosted on a special server somewhere on the Internet. I subscribe to the list by sending a message to that server—and when I say subscribe that means my name is added to the list of e-mail participants; no money is involved. Then I am able to send a message that gets copied by that server and sent to everyone on the list. I might post a question about training Jake or something that happened to him, and everyone on the list gets a copy of that e-mail message. Other people on the list might reply to my message and copies are sent to everyone as well. It's a means of carrying on a discussion on a favorite topic.

On the Internet, there is a mailing list for every interest. A site that catalogs them, *www.paml.org*, includes over 100,000 different lists on almost any topic you can imagine. Remember Jane and her Beanies? I'm sure she could find a few lists to join.

Newsgroups are another means of exchanging information or messaging on the Internet, but instead of the messages coming to us in e-mail, we must go to the newsgroups. Newsgroups are posting areas on a particular topic where the discussion builds over time.

Here's a way to think about newsgroups. Imagine a long hallway in a school or office building. On each side of the hallway are bulletin boards. Each bulletin board is devoted to a particular topic—gardening, diabetes, *The X-Files*. I might happen along and see the *X-Files* board and stop and write a brief message on a note card—"That was a great episode last night. Very scary! Where have I seen that actress in such-and-such scenes before?" Then I walk on down the hall. Someone else might come along and read the cards on the board, including mine, and write a response.

That's what the newsgroups are like—huge places to post comments and questions on practically any topic. There are over 50,000 newsgroups available! Remember I mentioned *www.paml.org*? You can find an equivalent site for newsgroups at *groups.google.com*.

Finally, there's chat. Has anyone chatted on the Internet before?

<Allow audience to respond.>

When we chat on the Internet we are accessing chat servers—sites that allow us to enter a "cyberroom" with other people in it. If I type "hello" and hit enter that message is displayed on the screens of all the people who are in that room. Our screen might include on the side a list of the people in the room, usually by their nickname or computer handle.

Instant messaging is another form of chat you may have heard of where special software sends private messages between two Internet users while both are logged on.

Slide 19: Functions of the Internet—Remote Login

Our second function of the Internet is remote login. That is where our computer connects to another and allows us access to information on that other computer.

One way people do this is through a telnet connection, such as logging in to our library's catalogue from home. Perhaps we might dial in to the local university to search its book listings.

A newer and much more popular form of remote login is the World Wide Web. When you hear people say they are "surfing the Web" that's what they mean. The Web allows us to log in to servers all over the

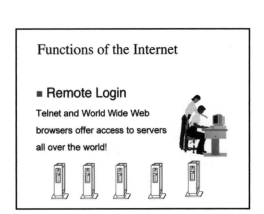

Functions of the Internet

■ Remote Login

Telnet and World Wide Web browsers offer access to servers all over the world!

world to explore or learn about almost any conceivable topic.

Functions of the Internet

■ File Transfer

Transferring files

- uploading

- downloading

- peer to peer

Slide 20: Functions of the Internet—File Transfer

Our final function of the Internet is **FTP—File Transfer Protocol**. FTP is the transferring of files from one computer—possibly a server out there somewhere—to another, probably your machine or a machine on a network.

FTP is a rather advanced form of interaction on the Internet and you'll probably spend more time on messaging and remote login than FTP.

If we send a file from our computer up to a server by way of a program designed to do FTP, that's called **uploading**. If we pull a file down from a server with FTP, that's **downloading**.

What might we transfer? We might upload some images or Web page files to a Web server. We might download an image file of a beautiful outdoor scene to use as a screen background from a public server that stores images and other fun "computer extras."

We might also get involved in peer-to-peer computing. Peer-to-peer computing involves the direct exchange of files from one computer to another, bypassing a file server. Have you heard of Napster? Napster is a **peer-to-peer computing system** that allows people logged on to search for songs they can listen to on their computers. Look for much more peer-to-peer computing on the Internet in years to come.

The Internet has many parts

■ Newsgroup Servers
■ Mailing Lists Servers
■ FTP Servers
■ Internet Relay Chat Servers
■ WWW Servers

Slide 21: The Internet has many parts

We've learned that the Internet has all sorts of functions. It has many parts as well. We really can't say that the World Wide Web is the Internet because the Net has a lot more to it. To review, here are some components of the Internet we've discussed as well as one we haven't.

Newsgroups, which are like the bulletin board systems, allow us to read messages by others on a particular subject. Mailing lists allow us to exchange e-mail messages with a group on a certain topic. **Internet Relay Chat** or **IRC** is yet another form of chat you can participate in by accessing special servers set up to host IRC chats. And we have the World Wide Web in this mix as well.

The Web is the slickest, coolest, most popular part of the Internet. It allows us to see colorful pages and images, hear sounds, and see neat animations and video clips. We sometimes equate the World Wide Web with the Internet because it's the hot spot right now—the thing everyone is talking about!

Slide 22: What is the World Wide Web?

So what is the World Wide Web? It is a collection of documents stored on Web servers all over the world. These documents are hypertext documents. Remember earlier when we looked at those addresses and discussed the hypertext transfer protocol? The *http* at the start of Web addresses? That means we are transferring hypertext documents.

What is hypertext? Hypertext is a way to use links to jump from one page to another. Links on Web pages allow us to click and jump from a server at the British Library in London, to a server in Seattle to a server in Australia and then back again.

Linked pages allow easy movement through over one billion documents stored on Web pages in the world. And that number grows every day!

The Web is also an incredibly popular new publishing medium. Web pages are up for huge companies and organizations as well as for smaller groups and even individuals. We see those addresses we talked about everywhere. I have seen them on the side of taxis, on billboards, on my cereal box, in the newspaper, in magazines, everywhere!

Does anyone here have a Web page?

<Allow audience to respond. Depending on the skill level of the group, you may have one or two or none. Here's what I usually say:>

What is the World Wide Web ?

- Collection of hypertext documents
- Linked pages for easy movement
- Popular new publishing medium

Well, after a few months of learning about the Web and surfing around it, you may be ready to have a page.

You may wonder why anyone would want to have a Web page? If you're in business, it's almost a given that you should have a page. For personal pages, it's simply becoming part of the community that is the Internet. Jane might have a page devoted to her Beanies. Some people have pages devoted to their favourite things: hobbies, celebrities, collecting, antiques, their animals. I have seen many Web pages devoted to someone's dog or cat!

Jake the Yellow Labrador

Slide 23: Jake the Yellow Labrador

<I have used Jake as an example for years in my teaching for the public as well as for library staff training. You may want to utilize an example close to you for this slide: your own animal, a friend's, or one of the many popular sites that feature canines or felines. You might highlight a page you find particularly interesting to illustrate the point of the Internet being a community. Other examples that will work: someone's collection, a page devoted to a trip someone took, or a fan page for a celebrity. You get the idea.>

Here's Jake—a yellow Labrador retriever who has had a Web page for over six years! Why does Jake have a page? Because his owner wanted to be a part of the Internet community where people meet and discuss their dogs: how to raise, train, and groom them. Jake's owner put the page up and has received many e-mails from other dog owners. This is simply an example of the global community I mentioned earlier.

Slide 24: Why is the Web so popular?

Why is the Web so popular?

When computers became more affordable and accessible, more and more people could get on the Web and check it out. If you don't have a computer at home, libraries fill the gap offering access to the Internet. You could visit our library or practically any public library in the UK and find an Internet connection, probably for free.

Our connections are faster and more reliable than they have ever been. ADSL and cable make them even faster as do the speedy connections found in most libraries and universities.

Our newer computer systems make it super easy to get on, look at a page, and follow links to others. You learned about the GUI—Graphical User Interface. The GUI is tailor-made for the Web. Using the mouse, you point and click and you are on your way!

The World Wide Web invites "surfing." I've used that term before during this presentation. Surfing is moving around the vast interconnected Web of documents and all of these servers we've talked about. Imagine a surfer climbing on a board and riding wave after wave to many different points. That's surfing.

> Why is the Web so popular?
> - Computers are more affordable and accessible.
> - Connections are faster and more reliable.
> - Graphical Web browsers are more user-friendly.
> - WWW invites surfing.

Slide 25: Web Browsers

Programs or applications called Web browsers allow us to surf. Your Web browser might be Microsoft Internet Explorer or Netscape. Those are the two big names in the browser business. You can use either browser to access the info on the Web. The information will be the same no matter what browser you use to access it.

It is important to remember that your browser is simply an application or program just like your word processor. It accesses the documents stored on the Web of servers and displays them with all their flashy colours and pictures and sounds and movies even.

> Web Browsers
> - They might be Netscape, Microsoft IE, or another browser.
> - You can use any browser to access the info on the Web.
> - Browsers are simply applications like our word processors or database programs.

What you'll find on the Web

- Government Information
- Consumer Info and Shopping/Auctions
- Entertainment/Popular Culture
- Current Research
- Online Communities
- News and Current Events
- FAQs

Slide 26: What you'll find on the Web

Here's a sampling of the types of information we will find while surfing the Web:

We'll have full access to government information, like the text of important bills and government publications and tax forms.

Consumer information, shopping, and auctions where you can find out about something you'd like to buy and maybe even a place or two to buy it.

Entertainment and popular culture is one of my favourites. Any movie, TV show, musical act, West End show, or the like probably has a Web page devoted to it with lots of useful information.

We'll also find current research on many topics of interest; online communities we can participate in, such as support groups or discussion groups; and a wealth of sites giving news and current events.

For many of these topics you'll also find something called a **Frequently Asked Question** file. **FAQs**, as they are known, cover almost every topic imaginable on the Web. We might surf to the FAQ on Labrador retrievers to find out about the breed or to the sinusitis FAQ to learn about sinus disease. There are a lot of possibilities.

WWW Caveat! The Web is *NOT*:

- Comprehensive in coverage
- A substitute for in-depth research
- Always reliable
- Censored

Slide 27: WWW Caveat!

I need to tell you that the Web is not the be-all and end-all for everything we do. It is not completely comprehensive in coverage or a substitute for in-depth research. Sometimes the young people we know think they can get all of their work done for a big report on the Internet. That just isn't so. Books, encyclopedias, and magazines are still around to provide well-rounded access to information. I should say, however, that the Web has made it easier to locate sources of information through listings of articles or citations.

The Internet as a whole is not always reliable. If something happens to our connection here at this library, we might not have access to the Web. Or if the server we want is very busy, it may not allow us to connect.

The Web is also not censored. You'll find a little bit

of something for everyone, as we said before, including stuff that might not be appropriate for younger children.

Slide 28: Useful Web Sites

Here are some useful starting points if you are ready to begin exploring the Web. The Webopedia will define computer and Internet terms for you if you come across some we have not defined here. And DMOZ is an excellent place to start your Web surfing adventures.

Useful Web Sites

- Computers and Internet Dictionary
  - www.webopedia.com
- Subject Guide to the Web
  - www.dmoz.org

Slide 29: Our Summary

And so we come to the end. Remember—you'll find some really interesting things on the Internet: a community of people who share your interests, a Web page about your favourite topic of all time, a mailing list to participate in, and a colourful, easy way to surf the world, and one of the fastest growing means of global communication. Thank you so much for your participation and interest.

Please take a look at some of the books about the Internet and World Wide Web that we have available for reference.

Questions?

Our Summary

- The Internet is a global community of people and computers
- that we can access via a network or from home with an ISP
- to browse the wealth of information available!

Module 3
Searching the World Wide Web

INTRODUCTION

Library users are eager to move forward once they have experienced the Internet and the World Wide Web. Searching for information is the next logical step. This module introduces users to the concepts of subject lists, Web portals, and the mysteries of search engines.

It's amazing how much searching has changed. As a trainer for the public and staff, I constantly remind my students that a subject list is not a search engine and a search engine does not search the entire Web. Recently, I discovered the wonders of the Open Directory Project (courtesy of an outstanding speaker at a Computers in Libraries conference), the emerging need to educate library users about portals, and the uncanny results of Google.

This module, as current as possible as of this printing, includes information on all of these topics to help your library users understand the nuances of locating the information they want and need on the World Wide Web.

Note that the Web evaluation module follows this one. I agree with Alexander and Tate who find this is the logical progression for teaching according to the Web teaching pyramid. For more detailed information on their ideas and research, please see *www2.widener.edu/Wolfgram-Memorial-Library/ pyramid.htm.*

WORKSHOP ATTENDEES WILL GAIN:

1. An understanding of the differences between subject lists, Web portals, and search engines.
2. A basic understanding of how a search engine creates its database with spiders and crawlers.
3. An overview of an effective method of Web searching: deciding on keywords, inputting, and browsing results.

TIPS FOR PRESENTING THIS MODULE

- As with other modules in the *Toolkit*, this session is enhanced by actually going live on the Web at the end to demonstrate the Open Directory Project as well as a search or two in one of the engines.
- The trainer might also allow users to do hands-on searches in a lab or library setting.
- Keep this module current; search engines change almost daily. Stay on top of changes, statistics, and news by checking in with *www.searchenginewatch.com* or *searchengineshowdown.com*.
- The trainer might also allow users to do hands-on searches in a lab or library setting. Practice questions can be found on the Web. Do a Google search for keywords "web practice search questions" or use some of your own favorites from working public desks. Some of my favorite SJCPL reference desk examples are:

  What or who is Ogopogo?
  Where is the Shaker community of Sabbathday Lake located?
  What is the address for the Ace Hotel in Seattle?
  Can you find an episode guide for <your favorite television program>?
  (I use *Absolutely Fabulous* or *The X-Files*.)
  Find a list of wineries in Tuscany.

MODULE 3—SEARCHING THE WORLD WIDE WEB—SCRIPT

Slide 1: Introduction

<Introduce yourself and your helper if you have one. Tell the group that you will be using a presentation program called PowerPoint to present the programme.>

> *Searching the World Wide Web*
>
> **Locating Information Via Subject Lists, Portals, and Search Engines**
>
> <Your Name Here>
> <Your Library Name Here>

Slide 2: Our Goals

Here is our class plan for this session.

We're going to look at how to go about finding information on the Internet, focusing on the World Wide Web and the wealth of information there. You have all probably spent time surfing the Web. Maybe you have wondered how to find a specific fact instead of just browsing around looking at pages. This class is designed to teach you searching skills.

We'll start with a look back at our discussion of the World Wide Web. If you have taken our *Introduction to the Internet* class, you'll probably remember a lot, but it makes a great starting point for this class.

Then we'll discuss subject lists, portals, and search engines. You've probably heard of search engines, but who's heard about subject lists?

<Allow audience to respond.>

Who's heard of a portal on the Web? That's a newer term.

<Allow audience to respond.>

Portals can be great! After we talk about portals, we'll focus on how search engines do what they do and how you can be a more effective searcher.

> *Our Goals*
>
> • Review: What is the World Wide Web?
> • Subject lists, portals, and search engines
> • How do the engines work?
> • Getting the most from your searches
>
>

What is the World Wide Web?

- Collection of hypertext documents
- Linked pages for easy movement
- WWW publishing a popular new medium
- Programs called browsers surfing the Web

Slide 3: What is the World Wide Web?

Here's our quick one-minute review of the Web. The World Wide Web is a collection of hypertext documents. Hypertext is a way of linking documents stored on computers all over the world. Linked pages allow easy movement around the Web from document to document. Because Web pages are easy to create, there has been a boom in World Wide Web publishing. We'll talk about how many pages there are on the Web in just a few minutes. Finally, programs called browsers "surf" or navigate the Web—you'll almost certainly use either Netscape or Microsoft Internet Explorer.

A Little History

- Subject list Yahoo! is born in 1994
- Search engines follow.
- Search engines and Yahoo! transform into portals in the late '90s.

Slide 4: A Little History

Here's a quick history lesson as well.

Back in the early '90s—that's a long time in Internet years—a couple of fellows at Stanford University in California, David Fellows and Jerry Yang, created a list of Web sites. The Web was pretty new then and there really was no organization. Fellows and Yang created what they called *Yet Another Hierarchical Officious Oracle*—or YAHOO!. YAHOO! was and is a list of Web sites organized by subject.

At about the same time, Web sites that specialize in searching for specific words on the Web sprang up. These are called search engines.

Portals came along more recently—sort of a "one-stop" site on the Web that might include many options for organizing information as well as searching.

Three Methods of Searching

- The WWW Subject List
- The WWW Portal
- The WWW Search Engine

Slide 5: Three Methods of Searching

All of these tools allow us to locate or search for information on the Web. Let's take a look at them one by one.

Slide 6: Subject Lists

Our first tool is the World Wide Web subject list. Subject lists are well-organized sites that allow you to browse lists of Web sites by subject or topic. Who's doing the organization? It's people. People create subject lists.

Subject Lists

- Subject lists are organized indexes that allow you to browse through lists of Web sites by subject or topic.
- Subject lists are created by people.

Slide 7: Subject Lists

Subject lists are designed for browsing. Using a subject list is like visiting a library with really good signage that points you the way to go. A sign says "here are the books on sports." Another says "here are the books on football." Another sign in that same area says "here are the books on professional football. That's what subject lists are like, but instead of books they point you to Web sites.

Subjects are clearly defined. If I am looking for a list of Web URLs for *The X-Files*, I'll probably move into the heading Television, into Shows, and to an alphabetical listing of all the shows covered.

Subject Lists

- Excellent for browsing
- Like visiting a library
- Clearly defined subjects

Slide 8: Who Creates Subject Lists?

Who creates these subject lists? Many libraries do. Just as we like to organize books and other materials, librarians have started organizing the Web.

Nonprofits are also involved, creating subject lists for very specific users—such as a subject list created for people who have diabetes. There are also notable subject lists being put up by organizations, like the Open Directory Project, which seeks to create the largest human-edited list of Web sites in the world. We'll talk more about that list in just a moment.

We also need to address all of the dot-coms putting up subject lists. The most notable would be Yahoo!, which has morphed into a portal as well. It seems like most of the for-profit lists have become portals. One

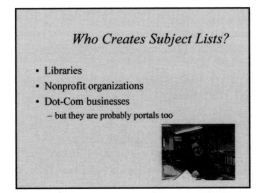

Who Creates Subject Lists?

- Libraries
- Nonprofit organizations
- Dot-Com businesses
  – but they are probably portals too

of the reasons for this is that the dot-coms sell advertising on their sites. The more traffic through their pages they can generate, the better.

A Sampling of Subject Lists

• Internet Public Library www.ipl.org
• Open Directory Project www.dmoz.org
• SJCPL Hotlist www.sjcpl.lib.in.us/hotlist

Slide 9: A Sampling of Subject Lists

Here are three of the many prominent subject lists on the World Wide Web. We'll take a closer look at a couple of these. In your handout, you'll find these URLs.

<You may want to replace slides 10 and 11 with examples from your own library's website.>

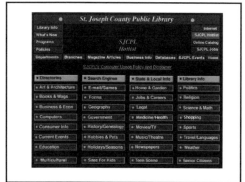

Slide 10: SJCPL Hotlist

Here's a subject list created by librarians for library users at the St. Joseph County Public Library (SJCPL) in South Bend, Indiana. SJCPL was the first public library in the United States to put up a Web page. They also got into subject list creation very early. It's called the Hotlist now. The list is created and maintained by staff members, who all bring their own expertise to the list. For example, a librarian who's really into science might be responsible for selecting and maintaining the list's section on science.

Annotated Entries by Librarians

BUSINESS—INVESTING—ECONOMICS

Slide 11: Annotated Entries by Librarians

If we go into one of those headings, we find a list of Web sites that have been carefully selected and annotated by the librarians. The annotation is that little blurb that tells users what the site is about.

For example, here's part of the business page. Note that each link has a sentence or two explaining it. That really helps library users find Web sites with information they're looking for.

The Hotlist isn't just for people in Indiana. Because it is on the World Wide Web, anyone can get access to it. The address for the SJCPL Hotlist is in your handout.

Slide 12: Open Directory Screenshot

Here's a screen capture of the front page of the Open Directory Project, also known just as DMOZ. The name DMOZ comes from the term Mozilla, a name used by the programmers and early Web developers for one of the early versions of Netscape. Mozilla is a little dinosaur fellow as well, and you'll see him at the bottom of most DMOZ pages.

DMOZ is put together by people all over the world who sign on to be "editors" for the project. If my favourite thing in the world is cooking chilli, I might be the editor for the chilli pages on DMOZ. Usually, the editor has some authority on the subject or it is a hobby or passion.

Take a look at this screen. Note the organization. It's similar to the St. Joseph County pages but maybe a little deeper. For instance, if we click on the Computer link—

Slide 13: Open Directory Screenshot

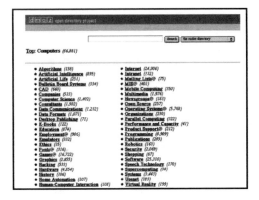

—we get a nice list of subjects that come under the heading of Computers. I might be looking for a list of links about shopping for computer hardware and software. I glance at this alphabetical list and find a link to shopping.

Slide 14: Open Directory Screenshot

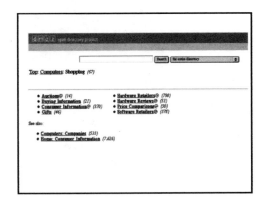

And look at this—even more choices, including buying information. It's simple to navigate through these lists to find what you want. If I went farther I would reach lists of links on that topic, and then taking those links, I would be pointed to various Web sites all over the world.

As you can probably tell, there is a DMOZ category for almost everything!

Note the search box on the pages from DMOZ. If you are looking for a particular subject, you can input the word or words and click on search. Results are returned from the DMOZ list: categories—such as cooking and shopping—as well as individual sites.

Slide 15: Subject Lists

Subject Lists

- Do not search beyond their user-defined databases -- if they search at all
- Do not allow advanced search strategies
- Sometimes contain dead links if not maintained

There are some limitations, however, to using a subject list. Subject lists are not searching the whole World Wide Web. That's an important fact to understand. A site such as Yahoo! is not really a search engine. Subject lists do not search beyond their databases—if they search at all. Remember that people create these lists of sites. Also, a subject list usually does not allow advanced search strategies.

Another stumbling block is that subject lists can sometimes contain "dead links" if not actively maintained. "Link rot" is another term for a link that goes nowhere in a subject list. The people at Yahoo! and at the library in St. Joe County have to be on the ball, making sure their links and lists are okay.

That can be frustrating if you're browsing around and find the perfect link only to discover that the page no longer exists!

Slide 16: Portals

Portals

- Portals offer a one-stop shopping look.
- Portals include e-mail, chat, auctions, news, weather, horoscopes, stock info, and more.
- Portals want to be *YOUR* starting point.

Our next tool is the Web portal, which I've mentioned already, but let's define it thoroughly. A Web portal offers a starting point for getting to different sites on the Web. Portals are usually like a "one-stop shopping" spot for everything you might want to access. Free e-mail, Web chat, auctions, news, weather, personals, horoscopes, stock info, and more are found on portals.

And—portals want to be *YOUR* starting point. They sell advertisements that are usually displayed along the top or bottom of the page, so they want to attract Internet users to their sites to see those ads. Have you noticed some Web sites allow you to configure your own version of their portal—like "My Yahoo!" or "My Excite"? A personal portal may include your local time, access to your local weather, your personal horoscope, and quick links to your favourite stocks and news.

Slide 17: A Portal

<Insert a shot of your favourite portal on the slide.>

Here's what a portal looks like. Notice all the sections.

<Explain portal features.>

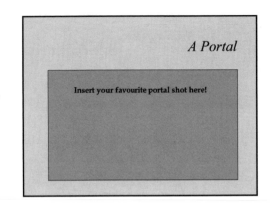

Slide 18: A Sampling of Popular Portals

Here is a sampling of some but not all of the popular portals on the Web. Have you been to any of these? Does anyone have a favourite?

<Allow audience to respond. Possibly discuss a bit.>

Has anyone configured a portal for themselves?

<Allow audience to respond.>

A Sampling of Popular Portals

- Yahoo! : www.yahoo.com
- Lycos: www.lycos.com
- Go: www.go.com
- AltaVista: www.altavista.com
- Ask Jeeves: www.askjeeves.com

Slide 19: Many Portals Began as Search Engines

Portals are newer arrivals on the Web and most of them really began as search engine sites. Our example here is AltaVista, which started a few years ago as an incredibly powerful search engine. Since then they have added more and more features and links and services—thus transforming AltaVista into a portal.

Many Portals Began as Search Engines

- In the late '90s, AltaVista was simply a search box and help area.
- Now it offers multiple services and info including translations and shopping links.
- Search feature remains.

Slide 20: So, What Is a Search Engine?

I've mentioned search engines a lot throughout our talk so far—but let's take a closer look and discuss what these things are.

So What Is a Search Engine?

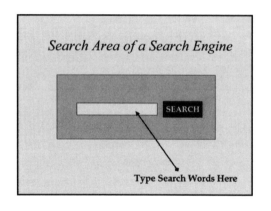

Slide 21: Search Engines

Search engines allow us to find words or subjects on a Web-wide scale by typing in a few key search terms. They search millions—if not billions—of Web documents for the words we specify and present us with a list of results or "hits." Some search engines are extremely simple, others allow various advanced searching techniques and logic.

Here is a key point: The database or list of indexed sites is computer-generated, not human-generated. The Open Directory Project and the St. Joseph County Public Library Hotlist are indexed and added to the pages by people. Computers create search engine results based on their internal logic and the user's query.

Slide 22: Search Area—Type Search Words Here

Here's a mock-up of the search area of a search engine. All of them—AltaVista, Google, Lycos, and so on—have different looks and colours. All will have an area somewhere on the screen to type keywords and a button to click to get results. Sometimes this area can get lost on the portal sites because so much is going on, but look closely and you'll see it.

To search, we can click inside the box to type search words—

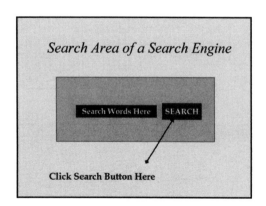

Slide 23: Search Area—Click Search Button

—and then click the button to get results. That button might say find, search, get, or fetch but they all mean the same: They send the engine to look at its list of indexed words to match your terms.

Slide 24: How do the engines work?

So how do the engines work? There is a lot going on behind the scenes of a search system, and it involves utilities or programs called spiders or crawlers. These are the automated programs that do indexing work for the search engines. They go out on to the Web and they look at pages and the words on those pages, building huge lists of terms.

Many of the engines also allow us to submit a Web site address to have a spider sent to index it. Recently, however, there has been a move to charge for submission of commercial URLs to sites like Yahoo! and Lycos. Many engines will continue to have that feature for free, though. If you put up a Web page, you might look at some of the engines that still allow you to add it for free.

> *How do the engines work?*
>
> - Search Engine Spiders/Crawlers
>   - Visit Web pages weekly or monthly to check for changes and new content
>   - Allow user-submitted sites to be added to their index

Slide 25: Search Engine Spiders/Crawlers

So, the big computer at a search engine sends out the spiders and they look at the text of pages. Some spiders do not go as deep as others do, looking only at the first bit of each page or just the top level. The top level might be the opening pages of a Web site or the first few pages of a multilevel site. Others might scan the full text of a page.

Search engines are increasingly likely to index the existence of multimedia, such as sound files or moving images, although of course they cannot index any of the data contained in those formats.

> *Search Engine Spiders/Crawlers*
>
> - Some do not go as deep as others.
>   - First 100 or so keywords
>   - The entire full text
>   - The top level of a site
> - Multimedia data is increasingly indexed as well, though not in detail

Slide 26: Rankings and Results

When we do a search, the search engine returns a list of results that will include the name of the page, the URL of the page, and a short bit of text from the page, containing your keywords or the introductory words of the page.

Relevance ranking looks at the number of times your search term appears in the document, in a ratio with some overall measurement of the document, like length or number of words. By doing what computers do—

> *Rankings and Results*
>
> - Search engines return a list of results.
>   - Name of the page
>   - URL
>   - Short sentence from page
> - Rankings are determined by the engine.
> - One click takes you there.

performing calculations—the significance of your term in the retrieved text is estimated, and the hits are given rank or "scores" that determine the order they are displayed. This is a rather complex approach, but it works well, staying behind the scenes.

Each of these results is hyperlinked—one click takes you there.

Questions? We've covered a lot of material already. How are you all doing?

<Allow audience to respond.>

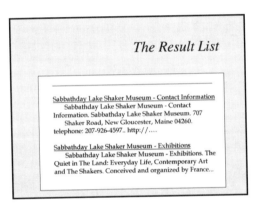

Slide 27: The Result List

Here's a typical search result page. Each result has a link, a bit about the site, and the URL. It's nice to see where you're going before you take that link. It would help you decide which link would be the best answer or source for your topic. This search was set to find the location of the last Shaker community of Sabbathday Lake. Note the first result actually includes the address in the sentence about the site—meaning I'll certainly find that information there.

Slide 28: Constant Change

Search engines and portal sites are constantly changing. From one day to the next, you never know if your favourite engine is going to change the look of its pages or the way it works. Search engine sites might, for example, add more and more portal features as time goes by. Unfortunately, it's never a good idea to get too comfortable with the way they look or operate.

Slide 29: Search Engines Are Like Cars!

Here's a great place to talk about this. At a library conference a few years ago, a speaker noted that we adapt to search engines like we do to our cars. We all have our favourite models—the ones we "drive" all the time, the ones we use to find what we need. Librarians have them and after you've explored the Web, you'll probably have a favourite search engine as well.

With the constant change we just mentioned you might find a newer or better engine to take over as your favourite. Just like switching cars every few years, we switch engines.

Slide 30: Some Statistics

Part of the constant change we mentioned includes the fact that the Web is almost infinite. It's growing at a phenomenal pace. In July of 2000, *USA Today* reported that there were 2.1 billion pages on the Web at that time. The article went on to say that there will be 4 billion by early 2001 and quoted a fellow as saying, "Even my dog has a Web page...."

That's true. A lot of people have pages for themselves as well as pages for their dogs, cats, iguanas, cars, hobbies, Beanie collections, photos, genealogy, and so forth. And more are coming everyday.

Some Statistics

- *USA Today*, July 11, 2000:
  - There are 2.1 billion pages on the Web.
  - There will be 4 billion by early 2001.
  - "Even dogs have a Web page..."

Slide 31: Some Statistics

It has been estimated by *www.cyveillance.com* that over 7 million pages are added to the web everyday: that's 81 pages per second. For an amusing, although probably inaccurate figure for the size of the Internet, visit the 'Irresponsible Internet Statistics Generator' at *www.anamorph.com/docs/stats/stats.html*.

Some Statistics:

- www.cyveillance.com reports the Web could be growing at a rate of 7 million pages per day.

  – *PC Almanac*, Winter 2000

Slide 32: 4 Billion Pages??

Four billion <or whatever the number is up to> is a lot of pages. There's no way that the search engines can get to all of them. A few minutes ago we talked about spiders and how deeply they might go into a site. Some search engines have more pages than others, depending on the programming of their spiders. Don't worry, though, because just about any of the major search engines on the Web today will return useful and reliable results.

4 Billion Web Pages??

- Search engines cannot possibly index all of them.
- Some go deeper than others.
- Useful results are common with most.

Slide 33: Rankings? The Best?

Rankings? The Best?

- www.searchenginewatch.com
- Pages indexed
  - AltaVista: 350,000,000
  - Fast: 575,000,000
  - Go: 50,000,000
  - Google: 1.2 Billion

So what is the "best" search engine? That's impossible to say, because they all have particular strengths and weaknesses and their individual styles. We all have our favourites that work well for us. Those of you new to searching will have your favourite soon enough. For now, however, we can look at rankings and statistics to learn a bit more about how the engines work.

A Web site that tells you everything you ever wanted to know about search engines is *www.searchenginewatch .com*. Here are some of the rankings from that site, according to how many pages are actually indexed by the spiders.

<These figures will change: you may wish to update the figures on the slide accordingly.>

Surprising, isn't it? That's a big difference in numbers, but that doesn't mean that one of these is better than another. AltaVista finds certain pages very well—lyrics, the text of speeches, and so on. Go might find many of the same things, while Snap will be strong with other types of pages. A lot of it depends on how each engine's spider or crawler works.

Slide 34: Google

Google

I want to tell you a bit about Google as well. It's a bit different from most of the other engines. It is not a portal at all. It is simply a search engine. As you saw with the rankings, though, it is a deeply indexed engine.

Google's front page at *www.google.com* has a very simple, very effective design. A box in the middle of the screen is for inputting your keywords to search. Two buttons below the box are labelled GOOGLE SEARCH and I'M FEELING LUCKY. That may seem silly—"I'm feeling lucky"? Instead of returning a result list, the "lucky" button takes you to the one site on the World Wide Web that Google believes satisfies your request. I have heard librarians and other professionals describe as "uncanny" and "spooky" how well it returns what you want.

Please check out Google sometime. It's engaging and intriguing, not to mention fast.

Slide 35: Getting the Most from Your Searches

Well, we've looked at how the search engines do their thing, but let's talk now about how you can be effective in doing your searches.

Getting the Most from Your Searches

Slide 36: Getting Started

Here are some hints to get started with searching the Web. These will help you if you feel a little overwhelmed by all of this information and the sheer scope and size of the World Wide Web.

Getting Started

- Learn about the various engines
  – including help files and FAQ files.
- Use search strategies -- "build" your search.
- Try more than one search engine.

First, learn about the various engines. You're already here in this class so you're on your way. Check out the engine's front page, take a look at the features, and make sure to read the help files and **FAQ** files. What is a FAQ? It is a document stored on the Web of **frequently asked questions** about a particular site or subject. The FAQ for AltaVista might include answers to such questions as "How does AltaVista rank results?" and "When do I use Advanced Search mode?"

The help areas will give you hints and tips on effective searching. For example, AltaVista is great for finding long strings of words or phrases if you place those words in quotation marks. I might use AltaVista to find lyrics of a song that gets stuck in my head or the full text of a poem.

Google, on the other hand, doesn't use any features like quotation marks. You'll read that Google wants nothing fancy at all, just your keywords, to do your searches.

Second, use search strategies to "build" your search. Think about what you are looking for and then think about the best, most specific words—we librarians call them keywords, which you've heard me say a lot in class. Use those keywords and any of the help tips you've gleaned for the particular engine you are using.

Finally, try the same search in more than one search

engine to see what different results you get. I've assisted library users with searching and they get frustrated sometimes when it seems like what they are searching for isn't on the Web. In fact, it may be that the particular search engine hasn't looked at the right pages. When we try another search engine or different keywords to see what comes up, we often get good results. We may all have our favourites, but it's a good idea to have a backup favourite if your first choice search engine doesn't produce results.

I'll remind you all, though, of something we teach in our introduction to the Internet. Everything is not on the Web. There are other resources available in the library that may help you find your answers.

Possible Search Questions

- Where is HMS Belfast stationed?
- What is included in the National Curriculum?/
- What's the address for the Robbie williams/ Fan Club?

These questions can be answered by using a search engine and appropriate search words.

Slide 37: Possible Search Questions

What answers will you find on the Web? All sorts of subjects are covered. Here are just a few questions that could be answered using a World Wide Web search engine. Take a look. What keywords might we use for some of these?

<Allow audience to respond. Talk a bit about each question.>

Search Strategy

- What is your question?
- What are the keywords?
- Input the terms.
- Examine the results.
- Try again if needed.

Slide 38: Search Strategy

Once again, here it is step by step. This is what librarians do and what experienced Web searchers do. Follow this course of action and you'll be a supersearcher in no time. These instructions are in your handout, so you'll have them with you next time you go surfing and searching.

Questions?

Slide 39: Beyond the Search Engines

Finally, I want to tell you a little bit about some other avenues for searching the Web.

> *Beyond the Search Engines*

Slide 40: A Note About Metasearching

Metasearch engines are sites that search multiple search engines at the same time. Have you heard of these? Dogpile and Ixquick are two of the prominent metasearch sites. At either, you enter search terms just like at a regular engine. The results returned are listed a bit differently. The result list might read: "Search engine AltaVista found 45 matches, displaying the first 10. Search engine Google found 76 matches, displaying the first 10."

What a metasearch site does is give you an overview of a whole group of search engine sites. It's a nice way to see at once how multiple engines cover a topic, and where your best results might be found.

Have these replaced regular search engines? No, not really. Sites like Google and AltaVista are still very popular on their own. It's nice, though, to have this option to retrieve that summary.

> *A Note about Metasearching*
>
> - Metasearch engines search multiple search sites:
>   - www.dogpile.com
>   - www.ixquick.com/

Slide 41: Specialized Searching

There are also other Web sites that specialize in searching for specific information or that search a specialized format of information.

Do you need to find an address and phone number for someone? Try the BT directory enquiry service.

For business information try the Yellow Pages. That site will locate businesses by type and name. I was able to find a listing of all the *<state type of business, such as Florists>* in *<location of your choice>*.

> *Specialized Searching*
>
> - People: www.bt.com/directory-enquiries/dg_home.jsp
> - Businesses: http://search.yell.com/search/DoSearch
> - Movies: http://us.imdb.com
> - Government: www.ukonline.gov.uk
> - Newsgroup discussions:
>   http://groups.google.com
> - Your library's leased databases

<Try this search before the class.>

For everything you ever wanted to know about the movies and people who make them, check out the Internet Movie Database at *http://us.imdb.com.* It lists practically every movie ever made and includes cast and crew listings and actors' and actresses' "filmographies." A filmography is a detailed list of every movie and TV appearance a film person has made.

For all kinds of information about the UK government, try *www.ukonline.gov.uk*, which provides an A-Z listing of all government departments.

To search newsgroups, *http://groups.google.com* is a useful site. If you are interested in how a certain topic was discussed in *http://rec.sports.football*, do a search in the Google newsgroup database and read through the posts.

For articles and newspaper information, check out what we have available at the public library.

<At this point, insert a short talk on what your library offers to the public: Ebscohost, Proquest databases, and so forth. It's always useful to get in a bit of self-promotion and let people know what you provide. In Indiana, the state library, the library cooperative, and government have banded together to offer all citizens free access to most of Ebscohost's offerings as well as some Gale titles. It's always fun to get library users interested in these options.>

Slide 42: Summary

All right, we've reached the end of our talk—we've travelled through subject lists and portals and talked all about the search engines. We've touched on the fact that the Web is growing incredibly quickly but we still have useful tools to search it. Thanks!

We certainly have covered a lot of information in our time together. I know we discussed a lot of terms like spiders and rankings. Don't worry. Soon this will all be second nature. How do you all feel? Are there any questions?

Thanks!

Summary

- The ever growing Web offers subject lists, portals, and search engines.
- Learning about features and practice will make you an info-superhighway master!

Thanks!

Module 4
Evaluating Web Sites

INTRODUCTION

We have reached the tip of the Web pyramid that Powell, Tate, and Alexander of Widener University describe in their work on teaching the Internet. (Their materials are on the Web at *www2.widener.edu/Wolfgram-Memorial-Library/ pyramid.htm*.) Please visit their pages for a scholarly, in-depth examination of evaluating Web sites in the library setting.

A must for librarians, these skills are important to the public as well. If we are providing access and instruction on surfing the Web, we must also provide guidelines for understanding what is good information and what may be questionable or based on opinion. The Web can be a virtual soapbox for anyone who designs and mounts a page.

I have presented versions of this class for librarians at the Indiana Library Federation meeting in Indianapolis and for local library consortia. Adapting it for public consumption forced me to remove library jargon and think not of librarians surfing for the answers to reference questions or for material reviews, but of our users looking for the answers to homework questions or other needed information. The best thing about this is that they are similar endeavors: remove the jargon and the same information applies.

WORKSHOP ATTENDEES WILL GAIN:

1. A basic understanding of how powerful the World Wide Web can be for locating information.
2. A look at sites that point surfers to useful information that has been selected or evaluated: the Open Directory Project, the SJCPL Hotlist, and the Internet Public Library.
3. An examination of points to consider when making sure the information you found originated from reliable sources.

TIPS FOR PRESENTING THIS MODULE

- This module reviews some of the points from Module 3: Searching the World Wide Web. You may want to mention that to your class if you've presented the previous module already.
- Do a search with Google or your favourite search engine for a medical condition such as sinusitis. Point out where the results are coming from: medical sites or sites that want to sell treatment methods. Arthritis is another condition that offers interesting hits to evaluate.
- Go live online either hands-on or in demonstration mode in your presentation area to visit some sites like those that answer the questions posed toward the end of the module: the Internet Movie Database, the Open Directory Project, or Google.

MODULE 4—EVALUATING WEB SITES—THE SCRIPT

Slide 1: Introduction

<Introduce yourself and your helper if you have one. Tell the group that you will be using a presentation program called PowerPoint to present the programme.>

Slide 2: The Web offers a wealth of information

Our question to address today concerns the wealth of information available on the World Wide Web, including all of the resources listed here.

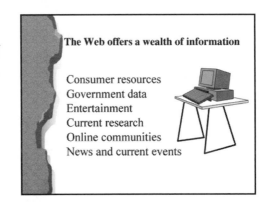

Slide 3: At your fingertips!

That information is virtually at your fingertips with a PC and Internet connection.

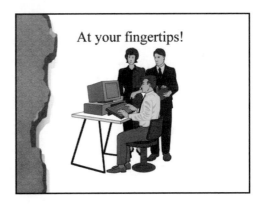

Slide 4: But how do we know what sites have good information?

But how do we know we are finding or looking at good information?

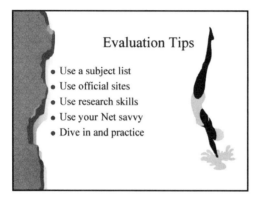

Slide 5: Evaluation Tips

You've come to the right place. In this class we'll examine ways to surf smart and get the most out of your time spent online looking for information. No matter if you are looking for information for a school project or just browsing to satisfy your curiosity, these tips will work for you.

Here is a breakdown of our plan for the class. Do these things and you're on your way to a worthwhile Net experience.

Slide 6: Use Subject Lists

Our first tip is to use subject lists.

Slide 7: Use Subject Lists

Subject lists are organized tools that allow you to browse through lists of Web sites by subject or topic. It's like visiting a well-organized library with signs that point you to what you want. In libraries we used to call them pathfinders.

Experts at subject lists evaluate Web sites for you, selecting them by using defined criteria. Well-made subject lists do all of our evaluation work for us.

Slide 8: Subject Lists

Here's a list of subject lists you'll find in your class handout. I'll invite you to take a look at all of these sites after class.

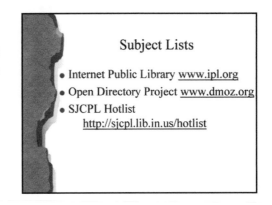

Slide 9: Internet Public Library

The Internet Public Library is a popular subject list organized by information professionals—librarians. The library is hosted by the School of Information and Library Studies of the University of Michigan. Librarians, as you know, like to organize and categorize things. The IPL librarians state part of their mission is to "serve the public by finding, evaluating, selecting, organizing, describing, and creating quality information resources."

Slide 10: Open Directory Project

The Open Directory Project strives to be the largest human-edited Web guide in the world, offering hundreds of pages on almost every topic imaginable. Note the major topic headings on the page and the search box for searching the directory. People from all over the world can become an "editor" at the Open Directory Project. If you have a speciality—if you are knowledgeable in a certain subject area, you can volunteer to edit the category of the directory.

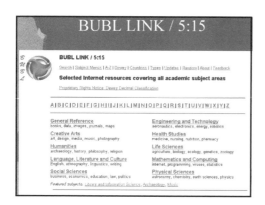

Slide 11: BUBL LINK / 5:15

The BUBL list provides a minimum of 5 and a maximum of 15 top quality websites in over 12,000 subject areas. It is a quick, easy and effective way to locate authoritative websites.

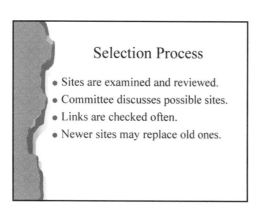

Slide 12: Selection Process

BUBL LINK is created like many of the subject lists on the Web: sites are examined and reviewed by librarians, who only include the most authoritative sites in any category.

Links are checked on a regular basis, bad or dead links are removed and newer sites may replace old ones.

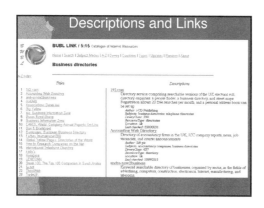

Slide 13: Description and links

BUBL contributors also write short descriptions or abstracts for the sites they choose. This is part of the business directories page at BUBL LINK / 5:15. Note the link to the websites.

Slide 14: Drawbacks of Subject Lists

There are some drawbacks to using just a subject list for information retrieval. The experts might not always be right at some sites, although the ones we just looked at have high standards and are well known.

Some links may be outdated and not replaced or deleted. You may find that perfect link for your search and discover the link does not work.

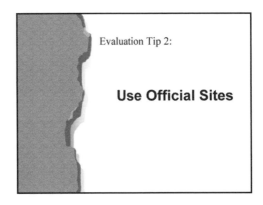

Slide 15: Use Official Sites

Our next evaluation tip is to use official sites.

Slide 16: Official Sites

Official sites offer well-researched information by professionals. Go right to the source if you have information needs. If I want to know all about the features of a new car, I might go to that car manufacturer's Web site. If I'm looking for a stereo, I might surf to sony.com or panasonic.com.

Official commercial sites are designed to interest buyers, so they will offer product info, comparisons, and list prices.

If I want to learn all about Diet Coke, I might go right to dietcoke.com.

Slide 17: A Sampling

For other types of resources like medical or government information, you might visit the official sites for organizations or branches of the government. The British Heart Foundatin maintains *www.bhf.org.uk*, which is a great resource for heart disease data. The National Association of Citizens Advice Bureaux at *www.nacab.org.uk* offers information and links about consumer affairs as well as a means to file a complaint.

Sites like *www.ukonline.gov.uk* present a subject list of links to different areas of our government. Transport information, grants, and tax information are just some of the items found on their guide.

Slide 18: Use the Expert's Tools

How are we doing so far? Questions?

<Allow audience to respond.>

Our next evaluation tip is to use the skills of experts.

Slide 19: Who are these experts?

Who are the experts? They're the information professionals, like librarians, who have developed ways to effectively evaluate Web sites.

Slide 20: Expert's Tools

Here are some of the elements we might look at if we were going to evaluate a Web site like the librarians at BUBL or at the IPL. Let's take a look at them one by one by asking ourselves some questions and then we'll have a little quiz. Are you ready for some quizzes?

Slide 21: Who created the site?

Who created the site? Are the authors of the page identified? Do they have credentials?

What can you tell about the person or persons who put up the site? Anyone can put up a Web page with the right tools and a place to store it. What makes the author of the site you are looking at an expert?

Look for buttons on a site that say "About Us" or "My Bio," click, and hope to get that biographical information. If you can't find out who the author is, be wary. I might find the perfect answer to a really hard reference question, but if I can't give a reputable source with the answer, it just doesn't work.

Is the site endorsed? Does it have backing by some entity you are familiar with?

Okay, let's have a quiz.

Slide 22: Quiz: Authority

I need some information for my report on Comet Hale-Bopp. I do a Web search and find some links. One page is called "Jack's Comet Round Up" and has a section on Hale-Bopp, but nowhere can I find who Jack is. Another page originates at nasa.gov and includes information compiled by scientists and researchers at NASA.

Which should I choose?

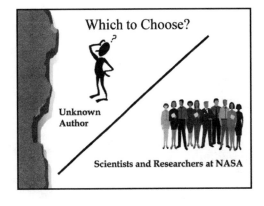

<Allow audience to respond.>

Very good!

Slide 23: What's the purpose of the site?

Next question: What's the purpose of the site? Is it informational? Commercial? Promotional?

Is the purpose clearly stated, such as in a link to a page concerning the site's mission or goals?

Some sites exist to sell you something. That's fine. Others are there to help you explore a certain topic, like medical issues such as cancer or arthritis. Can you tell the difference?

Time for another quiz.

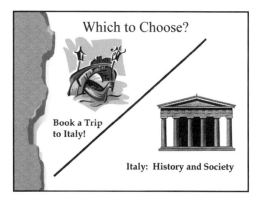

Slide 24: Quiz: Purpose

I want to know about Italian history. I just read Frances Mayes' *Under the Tuscan Sun* and would like to know more about the Etruscans, who lived in Italy centuries ago.

I search for Italy and get some hits. One site tells me all about planning trips to Italy and package deals I might consider to explore Tuscany for 14 days. The other originates from a university in Rome and details the history of the country. It contains a lot of pages and links to explore.

Which should I choose?

<Allow audience to respond.>

Very good! Any questions?

<Allow audience to respond.>

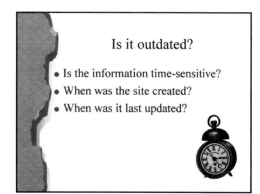

Slide 25: Is it outdated?

Is the site outdated and is that an issue?

Is the information time-sensitive? A government site may have mounted the full text of the U.S. Constitution in 1995 and not changed the page since then. That's fine because that document is static.

Time-sensitive information might be found on sites that review new computer hardware. I may be interested in a new CD recorder, find a great review for one, then notice at the bottom of the page that the review was posted to the Web in 1999. There may be better and faster CDRs available now.

Look for these clues: When was the site created? When was it last updated? Usually you'll find date information at the bottom of pages, sometimes with creation and update notes. It's nice to see pages updated often. Take a look at a category in the Open Directory Project and you may find that the page was last updated last week. They even note the time the page was changed, which is also very helpful in assessing currency.

Ready for another quiz?

Slide 26: Quiz: Outdated?

I have two sites to choose from to answer my question about weather patterns in the UK. One was mounted in 1997; no update is mentioned. The other has that information at the lower right of the screen at the bottom of the page. What might be a better bet?

<Allow audience to respond.>

Very good! Any Questions?

<Allow audience to respond.>

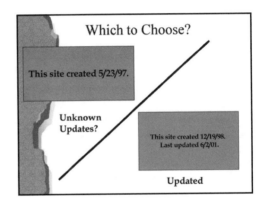

Slide 27: Is the site objective?

Is the site objective? Does it need to be? Some sites can present straightforward facts, like business sites that list their contact information. Other sites might cover topics that have multiple points of view.

Anyone can put up a page. Is that page serving as someone's virtual soapbox? In other words, does the creator have a bias? There are hate sites on the Web for various groups that present a rather skewed version of issues of race, religion, and sexuality. Can we look at a site like that and see their bias show through? Probably yes.

A candidate in a well-publicized, bitter election may use his or her Web site to present unpleasant facts about the opponent—are they really facts or are they a ploy to get votes.

Speaking of politics, here's a quiz about an election.

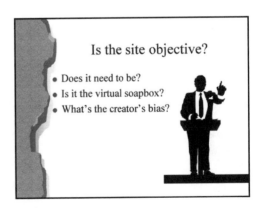

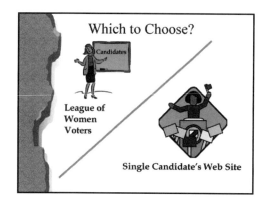

Slide 28: Quiz: Objectivity

I want some information about the upcoming election. I want coverage of the issues and the various candidates. Which site would be best?

<Allow audience to respond.>

Very good! But I don't want to dissuade you from visiting candidates' sites. They will offer a lot of background, contact information, and campaign news.
Questions?

<Allow audience to respond.>

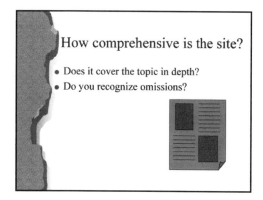

Slide 29: How comprehensive is the site?

How comprehensive is the site? Does it cover the topic in depth? Do you recognize omissions?
You may love to read and learn about the *Titanic*. You may be a *Titanic* expert. If you surf to a site called "The Official *Titanic* FAQ Site" that boasts answers to frequently asked questions about the sinking and discover that it includes no information on Captain Smith, the controversy over the ship that didn't respond to the *Titanic*'s rockets, or the discovery of the wreck in the 1980s, it might not be the most comprehensive site. You could surf on but still bookmark that one for what it does present.
Ready?

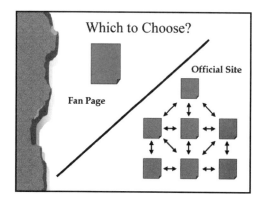

Slide 30: Quiz: Comprehensive?

I really love <your favorite musical artist, I'll use Stevie Nicks>. I want to see a really good site about her with current news and more. I search and find links to a single fan page with some pictures and a paragraph or two about her and her albums. Then I see a link to the official page *www.nicksfix.com*. It includes news, lyrics, tour information, and over 100 links to other pages. What's my best starting point to explore how Stevie Nicks is represented on the Web?

<Allow audience to respond.>

Very good! Notice I can still bookmark or use that fan page, but the official site is a great place to begin. We touched on that idea before.

Slide 31: Usability Considerations

You all did very well with the quizzes. Let's look at usability considerations now. Usability is defined as how easy or friendly a Web site is to use and navigate. That can be very important if you are working on a project and don't want to get bogged down in a poorly organized site.

Is the site full of jargon that makes it hard to understand, like too much techie talk or scientific terms?

Are there design flaws like misleading buttons, confusing navigation, large useless graphics that slow download times, and broken links. Outdated information plays into this as well. A neglected site will show its age.

Usability Considerations

- Jargon
- Misleading buttons
- Confusing navigation
- Large useless graphics
- Broken links
- Outdated info

Slide 32: Web-Specific Considerations

There are some Web-specific considerations. Remember that anyone can put up a page. Anyone with some cash and some know-how can also buy a **domain name**. A domain name is the top level address of a site, ending in .com or .net or any of the newer offerings like .biz or .info.

Domain names can be misleading and some unsavory Web citizens seek to confuse you. If I surf to *www.whitehouse.com*, I find a very explicit adult site. The official White House site is *www.whitehouse.gov*. Remember we mentioned NASA? NASA carries a .gov as well.

Web-Specific Considerations

- Domain Names
- www.whitehouse.com - Adult Site
- www.whitehouse.gov - Official Site

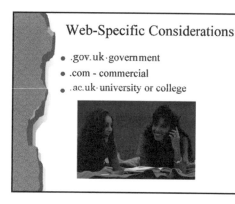

Slide 33: Web-Specific Considerations

No one but a government agency can have a .gov. Anyone can buy a .com. Most of those sites are commercial sites and they want to either tell you about their products or sell you something.

I might be searching for sites about the treatment of allergies and find I get results from sites like *www.allergyhelpforall.com* <that's fake!> that offer information, but their real purpose is to get you to order a bottle of pills.

The .ac.uk zone is reserved solely for universities and colleges. Students and professors get space on university servers, so you may think you're at a scholarly site, but it could turn out to be some student's personal, incorrect pages about a certain topic, like history or movies.

www.tametheweb.com/jake/

Slide 34: Web-Specific Considerations

Personal home pages are an important consideration. We mentioned the personal fan pages for some celebrities, but we might also find personal pages on all sorts of topics. The site may look great and may be fun, but is it good info?

Jake the Yellow Labrador has a fun Web page, but his page doesn't have all of the information we might need if we are interested in selecting that breed for our family pet. Jake's page might help, though, by offering "real life" examples of how Labradors behave on holiday or in other circumstances.

Be aware that a tilde (~) in a Web URL signifies sometimes that it is a personal user's directory on a larger server. A lot of colleges do it this way. That will give you a clue that it's a personal page on a .ac.uk or .com.

Slide 35: Use Your Net Savvy

Our next tip for the class is to use your Net savvy.

Slide 36: Know Where to Search

After you use the Web for a while, especially if you follow our other tips, you'll know where to look for certain types of information. Take a look at these questions. Each has a quick and easy way to find an answer on the Web. Of course, we could Web search all of them but sometimes you don't need to.

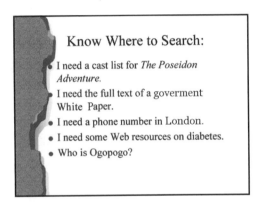

Slide 37: Internet Movie Database

I really want to find out who played Linda Rogo in *The Poseidon Adventure*, as well as other cast information. After using subject lists for a while, I've found many of them point to the Internet Movie Database for authoritative info on movies and television.

There I find a whole page dedicated to the movie, a cast list, and detailed filmographies for every cast member. A filmography is a list of an actor's roles.

Slide 38: Government Info

To locate a wide variety of information about the government you can look at this site, *www.ukgovernmentguide.co.uk* or you can check out *ukonline.gov.uk*.

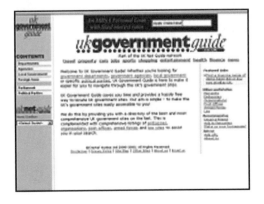

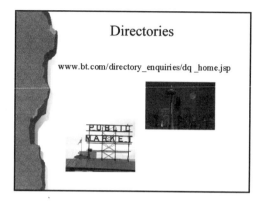

Slide 39: Directories

You'll also learn how easy it is to use Web directories for people or business searches. The BT enquiry service offers the full entries from all of the white and yellow pages in the UK. Have you used it yet?

<Allow audience to respond.>

I could find all the London numbers I need there, without calling directory enquiries. Remember, though, that this and other directory sites list only people printed in the phone book. If a number is ex-directory, it won't be found on the BT website.

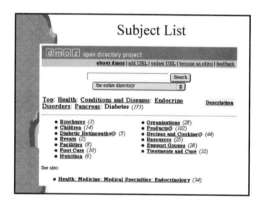

Slide 40: Subject Lists

A subject list is perfect for finding lists of sites about diabetes. In the first part of the class, we discussed that subject lists are put together by libraries and other organizations to offer useful, evaluated sets of links on a particular topic. Here's the Open Directory page for diabetes. This would be a great place to see all of the Web sites devoted to that disease.

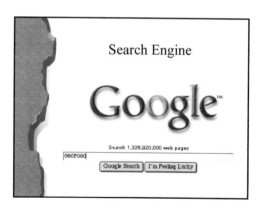

Slide 41: Search Engine

Some questions are perfect for a search engine. Who is Ogopogo? I might use Google and input that word to see what comes up.

Slide 42: Ogopogo

And here we see some Google results that tell us that Ogopogo is the Canadian cousin of the Loch Ness Monster.

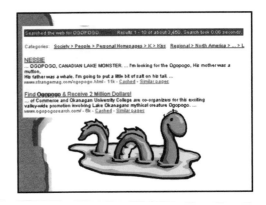

Slide 43: Practice, surf, learn!

These suggestions will help you become more comfortable surfing, searching, and evaluating information on the World Wide Web. The last one, read about the Web, means to look at books on the Internet as well as coverage in newspapers, magazines, and other sources. Many publications include sections on good sites to surf to.

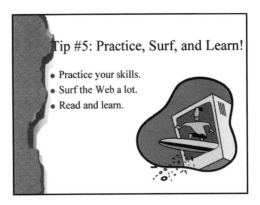

Slide 44: Thank You!

Thank you! Questions??

Module 5
Using E-mail and
WWW E-mail Services

INTRODUCTION

This module introduces library users to the world of e-mail. Probably the most used, most popular part of the Internet, e-mail is still mysterious to many new users. This module defines how e-mail works, what happens when we send e-mail, and what we can do with an e-mail account.

WORKSHOP ATTENDEES WILL GAIN:

1. A basic understanding of how e-mail works, including definitions of various components of an e-mail message.
2. An understanding of attachments, smileys or emoticons, and virus prevention.
3. An understanding of the concept of netiquette.
4. An overview of various free Web-based e-mail services.

TIPS FOR PRESENTING THIS MODULE

- The e-mail class is fun to do and incredibly popular with new users of the Internet. Seniors, especially, are very interested in learning how to use e-mail and how to get access, possibly through a free e-mail service on the WWW. This class presented with a hands-on component at SJCPL has pulled in many participants.
- This stand-alone class can be augmented by offering Internet terminal time to the class afterwards, like many of the modules in the *Toolkit*.
- Personalize this module as noted in the script below. Add your e-mail address, other addresses that are local (for example, change the Notre Dame address to a local university or your area's favourite school), and

any other addresses or mailing lists to make it more geared toward your group.
- Encourage participation. Ask the group who has e-mail. Ask what providers they use. As you move through this module, ask for examples of who they like to e-mail—friends, relatives, grandchildren, and so forth.

MODULE 5—USING E-MAIL AND WWW E-MAIL SERVICES—SCRIPT

Slide 1: Introduction

<Introduce yourself and your helper if you have one. Tell the group that you will be using a presentation program called PowerPoint to present the programme.>

Slide 2: Our Goals

Here is our plan for this session.

We're going to discuss exactly what e-mail is, how it works, and how you can get the most out of using your e-mail account by understanding some tricks and shortcuts people use. We'll also discuss netiquette. Have you heard that word before? That's etiquette for the Internet.

We will discuss how to get an e-mail account, including what to do if you do not have a computer at home.

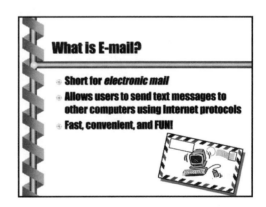

Slide 3: What is E-mail?

E-mail is short for electronic mail. It is probably the number one function of the Internet. How many of you have an e-mail account?

<Allow audience to respond.>

Good . . . and probably after this class those of you who don't will want an e-mail address so you can communicate with relatives or friends.

E-mail uses some of the rules that make the Internet work. Remember Internet protocols from the *Introduction to the Internet* class some of you may have taken? Those rules allow computers to exchange information—such as sending a text message.

Beyond all the techie stuff—e-mail is fun, pretty easy

to use once you get the hang of it, and really convenient.

Slide 4: Your E-mail Address

If you have an e-mail account, you get an e-mail address. Having an account is a little like having a post office box. When you give people the address, they can send messages to you. E-mail addresses are one of the two types of addressing associated with the Internet. They're distinguishable from the other type, addresses for pages on the World Wide Web, because e-mail addresses have the "@" (at) sign in the middle.

Your e-mail address is specific to you. Only you have it. It's like fingerprint. No one else in the world has your same address. If I'm <your name> *mstephens@whatever.com*, there can be no other mstephens at whatever.com. There can be an mstephens at **other** dot-coms or dot-orgs or the like, but only one at each.

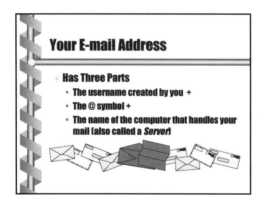

Slide 5: Your E-mail Address

Your e-mail address has three parts.

A username created by you or your e-mail provider might be a form of your name, like I might be <use your name> mstephens or mikes. Or it might be a nickname. If I were an antique collector, my username might be antiquefan. You set up the username with your Internet provider or e-mail service. It's at this point that the provider or service makes sure no one else on their system already has that name.

For example, the provider might say you can't use antiquefan because someone on their system already has that name. How about antiquemike or the like? Or they may offer to add numbers to your username to make it unique. I might be <Use your birthday> mike523 or mstephens523.

The next part of your e-mail address is the @ (at) symbol. That divides the username from the next part, which is the name of the computer that handles your mail. That computer is also called a **server**. Your Internet Service Provider or e-mail service has a particular name for their server—like aol.com for America Online or yahoo.com for those who go through the Yahoo service.

Who has an account with a local Internet Service Provider?

<Here discuss some local providers and what their server names are.>

Slide 6: Your E-mail Address

So here's the e-mail address dissected one more time— a username, the @ sign, and the name of the computer that handles or serves out your mail.

Slide 7: E-mail Examples

And here are some real life examples.

<Change these if you'd like! Try to include a couple of .coms, .ac.uk, and .org for the sake of the examples. Then use your address as the last one or the e-mail address of your library.>

We can tell a lot about a person's e-mail address by looking at the server name. We have some people here at .coms, someone at a .ac.uk—anyone want to venture a guess as to what university this person is at?— the US president at his .gov location, and an address at a nonprofit.

Finally, this last one is my e-mail address. See that it's made up of my username—<your username here> and the @ sign and the name of our server here at the library.

Slide 8: Advantages of E-mail

Here are some of the advantages of e-mail.

If anything, the cost of e-mail is very low. It might be just part of the cost of your monthly Internet connection. Or you might have a free e-mail account through a World Wide Web e-mail service. There are no per-message charges and no fees for sending e-mail.

Speed is another advantage of e-mail. It's actually pretty fast to send a message to someone. In the office, we might send a message to a coworker who will get it almost instantly. Or we could send a message to a friend or relative on the other side of the world that arrives in seconds.

E-mail is also very convenient. Any time of the day or night we can send off an e-mail message if we have access to our account. Our recipient does not have to be online for us to send a message to him.

With that in mind, it's also very nonintrusive. We check our mail when we want. We reply or choose not to reply when we want. It's not like a ringing phone that demands our attention at work or at home. There is junk e-mail, though, which we'll talk about in just a few minutes. That is one way e-mail might be intrusive.

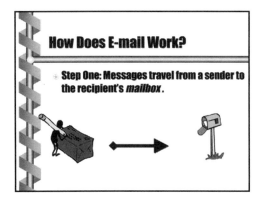

Slide 9: How Does E-mail Work? Step One

Let's talk a bit more about the mechanics of e-mail, so you can understand better what's happening when you send a message or check your mail.

When you send a message to your friend, it travels from your computer through your provider or service to your friend's mailbox, which is on her provider's server.

Slide 10: How Does E-mail Work? Step Two

The message is stored there on the provider's server until your friend logs on to check her mail.

Slide 11: How Does E-mail Work? Step Three

Hey! We've got mail! When you check your mail, it travels down from your mailbox on the server to your computer. You can call that downloading your messages.

If you are on a Web-based system for e-mail, it's a little bit different and we'll cover that in just a few minutes.

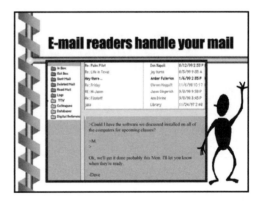

Slide 12: E-mail readers handle your mail

For now let's focus on e-mail use at home or work using e-mail software. **E-mail readers** are programs that handle your mail for you: composing, sending, receiving, forwarding, and all the other functions of e-mail are included. Readers are also called **e-mail clients**. You might use Eudora, Microsoft Outlook Express, or another e-mail program. If your e-mail reader is a little different from the one described here, don't worry, since it should have all the same features—it might just look a little different.

E-mail readers divide your screen into sections, including a space for your inbox, a window that displays the text of the message you are currently reading, and possibly a list of mailboxes or folders where you store your messages. Your inbox is where new messages appear when you check your mail. The displayed message is one selected to read. You can have many folders or storage areas for your mail. I might have a folder for mail from my boss and from colleagues, mail pertaining to a certain topic, and so on.

Some mail readers automatically check mail for you at preset intervals throughout the day or night.

Slide 13: Your Address Book

Another part of your e-mail reader is the **address book**. In the address book you can keep track of frequently used addresses and even have group addresses. I might store all my colleagues' and friends' addresses in the address book so I don't have to remember them. I might be able to just click on a list or key in a few letters of their name to get the address to pop up.

Group addresses allow us to have a number of e-mail addresses listed together. For example, I could have one called "Family" that includes the addresses of all of my family members. If I send a message to "Family," that message is sent to everyone on the list. "Hey, everyone, see you at the family reunion next week at the local park."

Slide 14: Your Signature File

Another feature of your e-mail reader is the signature file function. A signature file is a bit of text added to the end of every message you send that identifies who you are and whatever else you'd like to include.
<Use your own signature file or another example on this slide if you'd like.>

Here's Jane Doe's **signature file**. You might hear it called a "**sig file**" as well. Jane has her full name—she could have just used her first name if she wanted—as well as her e-mail address and her favourite quotation.

One of the most wonderful things about the Internet is the chance for Internet users to express themselves and be part of a community. A sig file that includes a short favourite quotation is a way to express your individuality. I have seen quotations from books, lyrics from songs, phrases like "Carpe Diem," and the like as sig files. Others have their complete address and phone information, like a business card.

You are not required to have a sig file or give out any information you don't want to, but should know that this is a possibility. If you do have a sig file, however, you should not exceed five lines—more than that is considered bad netiquette.

Slide 15: Sending a Message

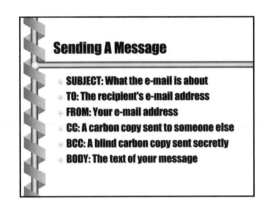

The most important feature of your e-mail program is the sending mail window. That window will have the following parts:

The Subject area: That is what the e-mail is about. The subject line is the first thing your recipient sees. Make it clear and descriptive.

The To area: Here is where you type in the e-mail address of the person you are sending the message to. Usually in e-mail programs you can put multiple names in this area, separating them by commas or semicolons.

The From area: Your e-mail address—automatically inserted by the program. You don't need to worry about that area.

These next features can be kind of confusing but very interesting.

The CC area: What is that? That is the way to send a **carbon copy** of your message to someone else. For example, I might write a message to someone I work with and CC it to my boss. That way my boss knows I have been in touch with the person. The person I sent it to can see I sent the message to someone else as well.

But the BCC is different. BCC stands for **blind carbon copy**. That means you can send a message to someone and a BCC to another. Your original recipient does not know that the message has been sent to anyone else. The BCC is used a lot in business situations. It's a bit sneaky. You might also use it to send messages back to yourself without your recipients knowing, if your mail handler doesn't automatically keep a copy of your messages. Some e-mail programs will archive every message you send if you set them up to do so.

The Body is the text of your message, where you type what you want to say in your e-mail. It can be as long as you need it to be.

Slide 16: Replying to a Message

When we receive a message, we read it and may want to reply to the sender. Selecting reply in your e-mail reader automatically addresses a return message to the sender.

When you reply, your e-mail program may copy the text of the message you received into the reply. That's so you can reply to different parts of the e-mail. You can edit this text just like a word processor does. You can delete as much of the copied text you want. Maybe you'll want to delete the entire copied text and write your own reply.

Also, when you reply make sure you are replying to the person you want to. If someone sends a group e-mail and you hit reply, you may be replying to everyone in the group as well as the original sender. I've heard of people getting in trouble when they reply to what they think is one person and it really goes to a whole bunch of people.

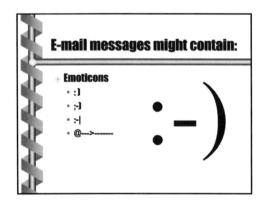

Slide 17: Emoticons

Here's some fun stuff. Have you seen these? They're called emoticons or smileys. They are little symbols made with your text keys to give your e-mail some humour or a personal touch. Here we have a smile, a smile with a wink made with a semicolon, a "I have no opinion" face, and—can you tell what that last one is?

<Allow audience to respond.>

Yes, it's a rose. You might send someone a rose in an e-mail message.

Slide 18: Abbreviations

We might also see abbreviations in an e-mail. Have you seen these? They stand for common phrases one might use in an e-mail.

    IMHO . . . in my humble opinion. That's a nice way of saying "here's what I think!"

    BTW is "by the way."

    LOL is one of the most popular. That stands for "laughing out loud." It's helpful for letting someone know you are being funny in an e-mail if it could be taken the wrong way.

    ROTFL? Anyone know what this one stands for? *<Allow audience to respond.>*
Yes, "rolling on the floor laughing." You might use this to reply to someone's joke!

Slide 19: E-mail Can Include Attachments

Well, we've talked about the different parts of e-mail and what might be included in a message: text, a smiley face, and an abbreviation for some phrase. E-mail messages can also include attachments. Attachments are files sent along with an e-mail that download onto your computer.

Slide 20: Attachments Might Include:

Attachments might include any of the following:

    Pictures: Images of the new baby or holiday snaps or scans of various photos. These will probably be in the file format of .gif or .jpg. Both of those are file formats made for images on the Internet.

    Documents or Presentations: Like a word-processing document or this PowerPoint presentation, saved and delivered in a particular format.

    Sounds or Songs: Small sounds can be sent as attachments for fun, to play on your computer or use in a program. You might also have a song of some type e-mailed to you in MP3 format. That's the current file format for digital music on the Internet that is causing

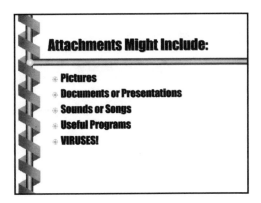

so much uproar and litigation. Don't worry, though, I don't think anyone would send you a song unless you asked for it.

Useful Programs: There are a lot of useful software programs out there that are freeware or shareware, meaning you can use them at no cost or at low cost. Someone might send you a little program or typeface or game or the like for you to use on your computer.

Now here's the somewhat scary part—viruses. Sometimes viruses can be transmitted through e-mail attachments. You may have heard of the "Happy New Year" virus. That's one that has been circulating as an attachment.

What can viruses do to your computer? If you get a particularly nasty one it may destroy some of your files or copy itself over and over until your hard drive is full.

How do you protect your PC or Mac from viruses while using the Internet for e-mail or surfing? Have a good virus protection program on your machine that scans your hard drive for viruses. Programs like Norton, McAffee, and the like are choices for virus protection.

Hoaxes and Chain Letters

E-mail hoaxes circulate the Internet rapidly
- Free Beer
- Free Money from Microsoft
- Sick Little Boy Needs Your Cards
- Infected Needles in Pay Phone Slots
- Viruses Will Destroy Your Hard Drive

Slide 21: Hoaxes and Chain Letters

Here's another important thing to know when you start using e-mail. **Hoaxes and chain letters** circulate on the Internet just like they do in the paper world. In fact, a hoax can perpetuate itself very quickly from sender to sender gaining more and more recipients as it goes along.

Here are some of the more recent notable ones. Has anyone seen any of these letters? They are all untrue! They exist just to be forwarded on by people who get fooled by them. Don't worry if you've forwarded a message like one of these on to others—now you know!

Any questions about hoaxes or chains? If you want to find out more about these, I've included some Web sites in the handouts.

Slide 22: Netiquette

I told you at the beginning we'd talk about etiquette on the Internet and for e-mail. That's known as **Netiquette**. Here are some tips for maintaining good behaviour when using e-mail:

Practice the Golden Rule—I like to say to people getting started with e-mail: E-mail unto others as you'd have them e-mail unto you. Use e-mail as a tool of communication. Rudeness will only breed more rudeness.

Don't type in all caps! You know what that means when you type your message in all caps—it means you are *<feel free to shout here!>* SHOUTING! In the world of e-mail and the Internet, a message or chat typed in all caps is construed as yelling. People might write back and ask why you are so mad.

No one can hear your tone of voice when you send an e-mail. Make sure your words are clear and well thought-out. Use the smileys we talked about or an LOL if you include a joke. Think of it this way: If I type "I have to go to the library today," you might not know if I am happy or sad about it.

"I have to go to the library today!" *<Say it happy—perky!>*

"I have to go to the library today!" *<Say it sad.>*

There's a difference. I'm happy about going to the library, so I might put a smile face after my sentence.

Think before you send an e-mail and please wait before sending an angry message. Some advice I've seen on netiquette says to wait a day before sending an e-mail in anger. Another rule is to never send an e-mail that you wouldn't want to be read on the evening news!

> **Netiquette**
> - Practice the Golden Rule.
> - Rudeness breeds rudeness.
> - DON'T TYPE IN ALL CAPS!
> - No one can hear your tone of voice.
> - Think before you send.
> - Wait before sending that angry message!

Slide 23: Spam and Junk E-mail

Have you heard of **Spam**? Spam is a bulk mailing of an advertisement for a product or service sent to hundreds maybe thousands of inboxes. Spam can really clog up a person's e-mail, just like junk mail, which is really the same thing.

Some e-mail readers have filters that allow us to automatically trash incoming messages that are perceived

> **Spam and Junk E-mail**
> - Spam: unsolicited ads sent to multiple addresses
> - Junk E-mail: unwanted e-mail of any kind
> - Many e-mail readers *filter* junk.

as spam or junk e-mail. Take a look at your e-mail software and you'll probably see some options for setting filters.

Slide 24: Free E-mail on the World Wide Web

Now that you know how e-mail works and what you can do with it, I want to tell you about getting e-mail service. One way is through an Internet Service Provider. If you sign up to get a home account, one of the things you get is an e-mail address.

The other way to get e-mail is to sign up with a Web-based e-mail provider. Here are a couple of providers you may have heard of:

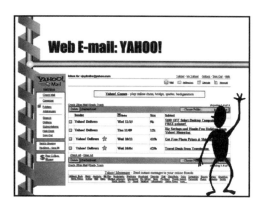

Slide 25: Yahoo! Mail Screenshot

The Internet portal and subject list Yahoo! offers e-mail. Here's a shot of their inbox. It's well-organized and easy to use and navigate. Now you can store messages in different folders—up to six megabytes.

Slide 26: Free Web-Based E-mail Services

Here's some info on these free Web-based e-mail providers. They use a Web browser like Netscape or Internet Explorer as your e-mail program. You don't need any special software, just access to the Web. That means you can check mail from any computer with a connection—home, work, travel.

I might be travelling for work or for pleasure. I could stop in at a cybercafé in London, for example. Who knows what a cybercafé is? A cybercafé is like a coffeehouse with lots of computers. People can have coffee or tea and surf the Web. Usually cafés charge a small fee to use the computers while having a beverage.

So at the cybercafé, I get my latte or chai or coffee

and sit down and open up Yahoo! or Hotmail and check my e-mail.

I might be at practically any public library in the UK and I can do the same thing, this time for free. I could be in Italy, exploring the Tuscan countryside, and come across an Internet computer in a café or library. I could check my mail and send messages as well.

These addresses will also go with you when you move. It's a reliable way to keep the same address.

Slide 27: Web-Based E-mail Services

You do have to sign up with whatever service you are interested in. Most will require you to fill out a registration form before they give you an e-mail account, including name, address, and birthday. They may also ask about some of your interests in hopes of sending you information from their advertisers, who make the service free to you.

The sign-up process requires some personal information from you, so it depends on how comfortable you are giving it out. They will never, ever ask for your national insurance number, your bank account number, or credit card number. If the free e-mail service asks for any of those, click away, and don't go back.

The service will also ask you to read their terms of use and agree to abide by them. Terms of use include promising not to send threatening e-mails to anyone, not to forward chain letters or junk e-mails, not to transmit viruses, and not to create a forged identity.

Web-Based E-mail Services
- Require you to fill out a registration form
- Ask for some personal information
- Request agreement with terms of use

Slide 28: Disadvantages

There can be some disadvantages to using Web-based e-mail. Systems sometimes are down or busy and login is slow, unreliable, or impossible. That can be very frustrating if you are depending on getting into your e-mail or if you're paying for a little bit of access in a café.

We might also note that it is less convenient than using an e-mail reader like Eudora. Functions such as filing e-mail or sending an attachment seem a little bit

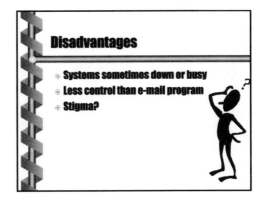

Disadvantages
- Systems sometimes down or busy
- Less control than e-mail program
- Stigma?

easier in a software program than on the Web. That is changing as our Web-based activities become more and more sophisticated and reliable.

Is there a stigma attached to using a free e-mail service? A few years ago the answer might have been yes, but now a Hotmail account or Yahoo! account is perceived like any other address.

Slide 29: Useful URLs for Free Web-Based E-mail Services

Here are some addresses for free Web-based e-mail. These will be in your handout as well.

For all kinds of help and information with e-mail, try the e-mailman.com page. For hoax information, check out Hoaxbusters.

Any questions?

Slide 30: Finding E-mail Addresses

The last thing we should talk about is how to find someone's e-mail address. Once you have an account of your own you may want to start writing e-mail to friends and relatives. The best thing to do is contact them and ask them. Phone them. Talk with your relatives at the next family gathering and collect e-mail addresses.

Another possibility, however, is Web sites that search for e-mail addresses. Here are a couple of notable ones. You'll find others out on the Web as well. I must tell you, though, that this is not an exact science. You might not find the person you are looking for or you may get multiple addresses for a name.

Slide 31: Conclusions

We've reached the end! Here's our summary: E-mail is one of the most popular functions of the Internet. We can send messages all over the globe for little or no cost. We can have an account with an ISP or Web-based service. We should remember our rules of netiquette—like never typing in all caps—what does that mean?

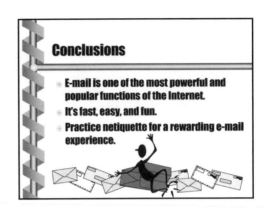

<Audience replies, some have even shouted!>

Right—shouting! Thanks everyone!

Module 6
Shopping the World Wide Web— The Internet Consumer Guide

INTRODUCTION

Library user interest in online shopping has grown in the last three to four years. In the mid-'90s, most questions posed at the Reference Desk at the St. Joseph County Public Library (SJCPL) concerning the Internet were, "What is it and how do I get on?" Recently, the questions have become more specific: "How do I search the Web?" "How can I find all the lyrics from the musical *Hair*?" and "I would like to purchase a book/CD/DVD on the Web—what's the best site and is it safe?"

Purchasing online, covered extensively in the news each holiday season, has grown from a mysterious, sometimes scary proposition to a multibillion pound pastime for Web users. Advertisements for online stores, big online savings, and the dot-coms fill the media. The year 2000, however, saw the demise of many of the start-up dot-coms such as those selling pet merchandise and deep-discounted DVDs. Left behind are the solid online stores that have become a brand name in and of themselves—think Amazon—and those entities supported with "brick-and-mortar" locations: Gap, Borders, Barnes & Noble, and many more.

My most important suggestions for people getting started with online buying: trust the big names and always look for an online coupon!

This module grew out of a series of classes at SJCPL on online shopping. Librarian Julie Hill and I first presented "Shop 'til You Drop" in December 1999. The filled-to-capacity class was well received—serious participants even brought their credit cards for some hands-on experience after the class.

WORKSHOP ATTENDEES WILL GAIN:

1. An understanding of what online commerce is, its origins, and current position in the consumer world.
2. An examination of the basics of Internet consumerism: an account at an online store, the shopping cart, purchasing, and shipping.
3. An overview of security issues and safety tips provided by the Better Business Bureau and other trusted sources.
4. A look at what types of sites are available and hints on how to find coupons and discounts.

TIPS FOR PRESENTING THIS MODULE

- Share your personal shopping stories: I have told groups about buying DVDs, CDs, and books, as well as having 40 pounds of dog food delivered to my front door for Jake. Have you done all or almost all of your holiday shopping online? Share that fact.
- One year, we printed multiple copies of a Barnes & Noble coupon that they had sent out via e-mail. BN encouraged the e-mail recipients to pass on the savings, so Julie and I distributed printouts to everyone in the class. They were delighted to take something home with them to use. Do something similar if possible.

MODULE 6—SHOPPING THE WORLD WIDE WEB—SCRIPT

Slide 1: Introduction

<Introduce yourself and your helper if you have one. Tell the group that you will be using a presentation program called PowerPoint to present the programme.>

> Shopping the World Wide Web:
> The Internet Consumer's Guide
>
> <Your Name Here>
> <Your Library Name Here>

Slide 2: Shopping the World Wide Web

Here's our plan for the class. We'll discuss many of the items you find at online stores. I'll explain how online shopping works for those of you who are new to the process. We'll talk about the reasons online shopping can be useful, and I'll give you some tips on effective shopping habits.

> Shopping the World Wide Web
>
> - What's out there?
> - How online shopping works
> - Why do it?
> - Seven habits of effective shoppers

Slide 3: What's Out There?

The Internet offers the opportunity to shop for all sorts of merchandise. Shopping sites are easily accessed from any PC with an Internet connection, at home, at work, or at the library.

How many of you have purchased online?

<Allow audience to respond.>

> What's Out There?
>
> - Today, the Internet offers specialized shopping for goods and services that rivals the largest stores anywhere!
> - Sites are easily accessed from your PC.

Choices

- Books
- CDs
- VHS tapes and DVDs
- Clothing
- Computer equipment
- Electronics
- Tools

Slide 4: Choices

The choices seem endless, don't they? I'm surprised sometimes when I hear of a new item that is available online.

Many of us may have purchased books or CDs online, as well as these other items.

<Present this slide and the following two slides as a means to interact with the audience. Ask them what items from each list they have purchased or tell them about the items you have purchased. This is where I might tell them about the 40 pounds of dog food I purchased for Jake that was delivered to my front door. I might also mention any recent purchases, and so on.>

Choices

- Gifts
- Household goods
- Linens and bedding
- Toiletries
- Prescriptions
- Pet supplies
- Eyeglasses

Slide 5: Choices

Choices

- Plane tickets
- Hotel rooms
- Rental cars
- Concert/event tickets
- Furniture
- Rugs
- And even cars

Slide 6: Choices

Slide 7: Other Sites

Other sites offer a different way to buy merchandise. **Priceline.com** allows you to name your own price for hotel rooms, plane tickets, and rental cars.

I might log on to Priceline and through a series of screens offer to pay £65 a night for a hotel room at a four-star hotel in Manchester. The hotel might be one of four or five listed on the site. Priceline takes the submission and then reports back via e-mail in a few hours if the offer is accepted and what hotel is providing the room. The same process works for plane tickets and rental car prices.

Be aware, though, that if you offer an amount and it is accepted, you are obligated to complete the transaction and accept the service. You give your credit card number when making the offer so you are locked in to the transaction.

Other Sites

- www.priceline.com
  - Allows you to name a price for hotel rooms, plane tickets, and rental cars

Slide 8: Other Sites

Auction sites such as **eBay™** have become popular in the last few years as a way for buyers and sellers to meet and exchange goods. Buyers bid on items and win if they make the highest bid. The auction sites are like huge virtual car-boot sales.

<If you are planning to present the Auctions module of the Toolkit, plug that class here.>

Other Sites

- Auction Sites such as www.ebay.com
  - Allow buyers and sellers to meet and exchange goods
  - Are huge virtual car-boot sales

Slide 9: Other Sites

A Web site called **NetFlix** has offered online DVD rentals for over two years. They have made it very easy to rent all sorts of DVD titles from your computer. If it's on DVD, this site probably offers it.

You select DVDs and they are shipped to you through the mail. You can keep the DVD for as long as you want. After viewing, you mail the DVD back in a mailer NetFlix supplies. Various set fees or plans are available. The most popular plan allows you unlimited rentals each month for about $20, with a limit of four out at any one time. Unfortunately this is an American site,

Other Sites

- Online DVD rentals at www.netflix.com
  - Huge selection
  - Unlimited time
  - Set monthly fees

but one or two sites in the UK are beginning to offer this service as well, such as *www.rent-a-dvd.co.uk*.

Consumer Reports
Best Stuff to Buy Online

- Books
- Music and movies
- Toys
- Software
- Computers
- Electronics
- Brand name clothing

Slide 10: Consumer Reports *Best Stuff to Buy Online*

Consumer Reports listed the best stuff to buy online in January of 2001. This list reflects the most popular items purchased as well as the items that have the best value when purchased online.

<You may also wish to refer to 'Which Online' at www.which.net —the site provides useful information on buying online, with a list of trades to subscribe to their Web Trader Scheme.>

Some Statistics

- **PC Data Online**
  - Christmas Period spending 1999 : $4.7 Billion
  - Christmas Period spending 2000 : $9.8 Billion
- **Business Week**
  - Amazon ships 31 million units in November and December
  - Possible quarterly sales of $1 Billion

Slide 11: Some Statistics

<Update this slide as needed. Newer information will be available as the Toolkit *is published.>*

Here are some statistics:

Christmas period sales online in 1999 topped out at $4.7 billion but more than doubled for the same season in 2000, according to PC Data Online, a popular Web site that monitors electronic commerce.

Business Week reported that e-tailer **Amazon** shipped 31 million units during the Christmas season, 50 percent more than in 1999. Their sales for the last quarter of 2000 were predicted to be around $1 billion—a large percentage of the total number above.

That's an impressive amount of sales and units shipped.

Recent Changes

- Brick-and-Mortar stores go online
- Dot-com becomes dot-carnage
- Sales still on the increase

Visit Us Online!

Slide 12: Recent Changes

The last couple of years saw many established stores go online in response to the boom of Internet commerce. **Brick-and-Mortar** is a term used to describe businesses that have physical buildings. **Click-and-Mortar** or **bricks-and-clicks** are newer terms that apply to established merchants who have built a presence on the Web.

The dot-com boom slowed in 1999 and 2000 as well. Some of the news media in places like Seattle and the Silicon Valley dubbed the dot-com slowdown dot-carnage or dot-bomb as many online merchants were forced to shut down and release employees due to depleted start-up funds. Even Amazon released over 1,000 employees in January of 2001 after their holiday season.

Even with this shift, online sales are still on the increase as big names go online.

Slide 13: "Click-and-Mortar"

Some well-known consumer giants now have Web sites devoted to shopping. They can heavily promote the sites inside their actual stores, urging shoppers to browse their online offerings any time of the day or night.

Big names like Harrods and Tesco have recognized the need to offer a cybercounterpart to their locations in towns and shopping centres.

> "Click-and-Mortar"
>
> - www.tesco.com
> - www.harrods.com
> - www.whsmith.co.uk
> - www.comet.co.uk
> - www.dixons.co.uk

Slide 14: "Click-and-Mortar"

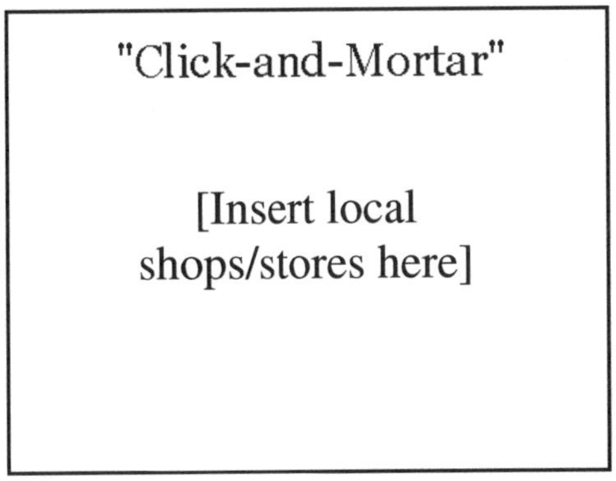

Of course, not only large companies can be found online: even local companies and organizations now have an Internet presence.

<Use some examples of local shops here.>

> "Click-and-Mortar"
>
> [Insert local shops/stores here]

Online Shopping Sites 101

- Most online stores have
  - Catalogue of goods/product info
  - Carts to store selected items
  - Secure checkout area
  - Accounts for each shopper

Slide 15: Online Shopping Sites 101

No matter what Web site you are shopping at, most of the sites have many of the same features. At whatever retailer's site, shoppers will find access to the catalogue of merchandise, "carts" to store selected items for purchase, and a secure checkout area. Shoppers will also be able to establish an account with the online retailer to manage orders and pay for purchases.

Let's look at the online shopping basics a bit more closely.

Catalogue of Goods/Product Info

- Images
- Product descriptions
- Styles
- Sizes
- Colours

Slide 16: Catalog of Goods/Product Info

We might log on to a well-known retailer, perhaps Amazon, Tescos, or Borders. We are given a start page or homepage that includes current deals and merchandise highlights as well as a search area to locate items we'd like to buy. That search mechanism gives us access to their complete **catalogue** of products, including detailed product information.

We'll probably get an image of the item that lets us see the cover art of the book or CD or a picture of the item. Viewing images is very handy for online shopping. This is especially useful for other types of online retailers, such as clothes manufacturers, where you can see exactly how a jumper or pair of trousers looks.

Product descriptions also help us decide if the item is right for us. Does the CD have on it the songs we want? Does the book's description meet our needs? Does the portable CD player have enough features?

We might browse various styles of clothing available at a site. A jumper might be V-neck, crew neck, mock turtle, or turtleneck. Each might have a photo so we could decide which we liked better. Some sites even create a virtual model to show how clothes or shoes will look. One site, eyeglasses.com, in the USA, offers the chance to see how frames will look on your own face if you submit a digital picture to them.

Sizes are usually detailed in the product descriptions as well. Some items of clothing might be available only in certain sizes. Further information on measurements and sizes can be found by browsing help pages at certain online clothiers.

An online product description will also give you a listing or even small images of the available colours of an item. The portable MiniDisc player available from Sony online might come in three different shades: metallic blue, red, or black. An image would help us decide.

Slide 17: "Carts" Store Selected Items

As we browse around a shopping site, we can put aside selected items that we want to purchase in an **electronic shopping cart**. Usually, we click on a checkbox or button to put the item into a cart, or holding area, until final checkout. These cybercarts can be saved for later purchase, edited as needed, and completely emptied if we decide not to purchase at all.

The cart displays like any Web page. In it we can change the quantity of a certain item, choosing, for example, to purchase two copies of the new John Grisham novel instead of one. Or we can see what our subtotal is on some sites by viewing the cart.

> ### "Carts" Store Selected Items
>
> - Usually a checkbox or button puts the item into your personal shopping cart
> - Carts can be
>   - Saved
>   - Edited
>   - Emptied

Slide 18: Secure Checkout Area

When we have finished adding items to our cart, we are ready to move to the **checkout area** of the site. Usually there is a button on the cart page somewhere that reads "Checkout Now." Clicking there moves the cart into a secure area where we enter name, shipping address, and payment information. Usually that means a credit card number. Some sites, however, do allow you to create an order and then mail a check to the company to receive your order, or phone in your credit card information.

Finally, in this secure area a purchase confirmation screen appears when your order is accepted. This screen can be printed for your records. It usually contains a list of your ordered items and the purchase price with information on shipping. This information may also be sent to you via an e-mail.

> ### Secure Checkout Area
>
> - When you are ready to purchase
>   - Cart is moved into secure area
>   - Shipping address is entered
>   - Payment information is entered
>   - Purchase confirmation is provided

Accounts for Each Shopper

- You establish an account that
  - Keeps track of order histories
  - Stores your shipping/payment information
  - Remembers you next time

Slide 19: Accounts for Each Shopper

At most of the big Web shopping sites, we establish an **account** when we place our first order. That account is updated each time we use the site. Accounts keep track of our order histories, probably going back to our very first order. Some sites store our shipping and payment information in a secure account area so we don't have to keep typing in our address each time we order.

Some of the sites actually remember users each time they visit because of something called a **cookie**. A cookie is a little file of information a shopping site places on your hard drive that it looks at each time you log on to that site. That way, the start screen of Amazon, for example, might read "Welcome Back, Jane" or "Welcome Back, Joe."

Security and Cookies

- Well-known sites are secure.
- Make sure checkout is secure.
- Set your browser to alert you.
- You choose to accept cookies.

Slide 20: Security and Cookies

Let's discuss security and cookies a bit more. This is sometimes the thing that keeps people from shopping online.

A well-known, well-publicized site like Amazon or any of the others in the presentation or on your handouts will always have secure checkout. In fact, any site that's really interested in earning trust and therefore gaining business will. Secure means the transmission of your credit card number and other personal information is encrypted, or coded, when it travels from your PC to the shopping site's server so that it can't be captured and read by anyone except the intended receiver.

If in doubt at a certain shopping site, you can make sure that your checkout is secure by setting your browser to alert you when you enter and leave a secure part of the site. Various browsers do that differently. Take a look at your browser's preferences to find out more. A secure area of a Web site will also have an address that begins with *https://*. The S stands for security.

In your browser preferences you can also select options to accept or not accept cookies. Most cookies are really very helpful, especially when shopping online.

It's the cookie that also remembers items left in your cart that you wanted to save until next time. But if you have a real problem with a company collecting this kind of data, you can set it to not accept.

Slide 21: Why Shop Online?

Why shop online? Prices are sometimes very good. Online stores are open 24 hours a day, seven days a week. The selection at many sites, especially for books and music, can be much larger than our local stores. And, if you have ever circled a shopping centre at Christmas time in your car, think about the ease of shopping without driving or parking first.

Seriously, as noted before, online shopping brings a wealth of merchandise to rural areas where some items can't be found. It also allows us to shop in slippers and pyjamas in the middle of the night.

> **Why Shop Online?**
>
> - Prices
> - Ease of use - anytime, anywhere
> - Selection
> - You don't need to find a parking spot!
>
>

Slide 22: Seven Habits of Effective Online Shoppers

Here are some tips to help you get the most out of your online shopping experience. These are culled from the Better Business Bureau's Web site, television appearances by Jean Chatzky of *Money* magazine, and issues of *Consumer Reports*.

> **Seven Habits of Effective Online Shoppers**
>
> - The Better Business Bureau, Jean Chatzky of *Money* magazine, and *Consumer Reports* offer shoppers the following tips to ensure that your cybershopping experience is a satisfying one:

Slide 23: Habit #1

Habit #1: Use comparison sites and shopping bots wisely.

A comparison site or shopping robot automatically goes out onto the Web and checks prices for an item, returning a listing of the best deals available. This is a wise way to shop to make sure you are getting the most for your pound. It's very similar to searching with a search engine. Instead of keywords, we use shopping bots to search for the best prices.

Sites like mysimon.com specialize in assisting shop-

> **Habit #1**
>
> - Use comparison sites and shopping robots wisely.
>   - www.mysimon.com
>   - www.bottomdollar.com

pers. You might look for the new John Grisham novel there and get a range of prices from £10 to £15 at different Web retailers.

Slide 24: Habit #2

Habit #2: Watch those shipping costs.

You may find a CD for £8 but shipping and handling at the shopping site adds £3. Another site may have the same CD for £10 with free shipping or perhaps £1 shipping. It pays to use the shopping robots and to compare shipping prices yourself.

Many sites will offer added services, such as gift wrapping for Christmas or other occasions. You can key in what you'd like the gift card to read and that text will be printed on a card with the gift. Be aware, though, that these extra services can increase your shipping and handling costs.

Also, if you order more than one item, some sites will ship each item individually if they are not all in stock at the time of order. You'll pay shipping on each item that way. Look for an option to ship the order only when all items are in stock.

Slide 25: Habit #3

Habit #3: Determine the company's refund and return policies before you place an order.

Some sites require you to ship unwanted merchandise back yourself or contact them for a return authorization. Some sites will allow you to return merchandise with a prepaid mailer they supply. Some sites that have "brick-and-mortar" stores will allow you to return the items there for store credit.

I might buy an outfit from the Gap online but find that it doesn't fit like I thought it would. I can return it to the Gap store at the mall because of their return policies.

Slide 26: Habit #4

Habit #4 : Always use a credit card to order.

It's really not risky to pay with a credit card online. In fact, because of the encryption that sites use, it's very safe. Recently, many credit card services are even offering more protection for online buyers. Check with your credit card company for more information.

Habit #4

• Always use a credit card to order.

£

Slide 27: Habit #5

Habit #5: Save a copy of your confirmation/receipt.

When that confirmation screen comes up, save it to your hard drive or click on the print button in your browser or both. Put the sheet in a safe place. This will protect you if your order is lost or if you receive the wrong merchandise. That confirmation will probably include an order number that the support people at the shopping site can use to track your order or issue you a refund or exchange. I keep my confirmations until I receive the order.

Habit #5

• Save a copy of your confirmation/receipt.

Slide 28: Habit #6

Habit #6: Order from secure, well-known businesses and establish a relationship.

This is a most important habit. Make sure the site you are ordering from is secure. We mentioned that before. Make sure the site is well known. That ensures they will have secure ordering and fair return policies.

Establish a relationship, as well, by taking advantage of e-mail offers and sales. You'll save money and maybe receive special deals and discounts for good customers.

Habit #6

• Order from secure, well-known businesses and establish a relationship.

Habit #7

- Shop with a coupon/discount if possible or use charitable portals.

Slide 29: Habit #7

Habit #7: Shop with a coupon/discount if possible.

Our last habit is one of my favourites. Look around the Web for valuable coupons for your favourite online merchants. You might save a few dollars or receive free shipping.

Some companies will offer you a discount if you buy online, or book a train ticket, or order insurance, for example. Always check out an online store just to see if you can obtain a few pounds off a product.

Sites like greatergood.com are portals to the world of online shopping as well as sites that benefit from your passing through them. For example, if we surf to greatergood.com and click on their link to Amazon, up to 15 percent of our purchase is donated to a list of various charities such as Special Olympics.

More Tips for Shoppers

- Visit www.shopsafe.co.uk
- Visit various consumer sites.
- Search for product reviews before buying.
- Let technology work for you.

Slide 30: More Tips for Shoppers

Here are a few more tips for serious Web shoppers. Visit the Web sites listed here and in your handouts, and search the Internet for product reviews before buying.

Let the amazing technology, like shopping robots, work for you. Stay on top of what's happening with online commerce because the technology will always improve the experience. Someday, your personal shopping assistant may appear on your screen to announce a big sale on your favourite item from Harrods or that new release from Stephen King.

Slide 31: Thanks!

Thanks for your attention. What questions do you have about online shopping?

Thanks!

Questions?

Module 7
Planning and Maintaining a Web Site for Small Business, Organizations, or Personal Use

INTRODUCTION

Library users who have embraced the Web, attended as many classes as possible at the library, and mastered the ins and outs of searching and evaluating information on the Internet may be ready to put up their own Web page. This module is for them.

"An Introduction to HTML" and "Designing and Maintaining a Website" are my favourite classes to present at the St. Joseph County Public Library (SJCPL)—because participants are *serious* about the subject matter and are probably familiar with the basics. Class discussions, questions, and sharing of participants' experiences with Web design make it an incredibly rewarding class.

This module presents the most pertinent information in planning and designing a Web site. Cost, graphic design, HTML, and organization are key elements of this class.

Who is your audience? Probably small business owners, people who work with nonprofits, or those interested in putting up a personal page. My most recent presentation of this class included a woman designing pages for her church, a gentleman putting up his tyre business, and a young couple interested in sharing their collection of antique books with the world.

WORKSHOP ATTENDEES WILL GAIN:

1. An understanding of the key steps to begin planning a site: examining other pages, exploring page layout schemes, and diagramming.
2. An overview of the costs involved in creating and making a page available on the WWW: domain fees, ISP hosting, design fees, graphics, and more.
3. An action plan for developing their own site and pointers to Web resources and books that will help.

TIPS FOR PRESENTING THIS MODULE

- Let the participants talk as long as you feel comfortable. I have found myself facilitating some great discussions with a group about getting on the Web. I try to allow extra class time for this purpose.
- Promote this class as advanced—not for the beginner. It would be best if your participants have been through the other classes in this book or taken similar classes offered at your library. At SJCPL, this has been one of the few classes where the class brochure states that it is advanced and not for first-timers.

MODULE 7—PLANNING AND MAINTAINING A WEB SITE FOR SMALL BUSINESS, ORGANIZATIONS, OR PERSONAL USE—SCRIPT

Slide 1: Introduction

<Introduce yourself and your helper if you have one. Tell the group that you will be using a presentation program called PowerPoint to present the programme.>

Slide 2: The mime is ready.

In this class we're going to discuss all the elements of creating a Web page or Web site. Here's our friend who may be like some of you. He'll be with us as we move through all of this information.

Who is ready to publish a page on the Web? Would anyone like to share what type of site? A business? An organization? A personal interest?

<Allow audience to respond. Interact a bit with them if they seem willing to talk.>

Slide 3: The mime is puzzled.

What we'll talk about tonight are the steps you need to take to make your wish for a spot on the Web a reality. Keep your personal goals in mind as we talk about each step in the process.

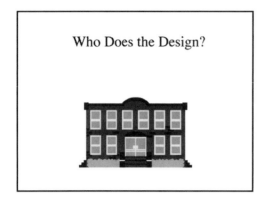

Slide 4: Who Does the Design?

First, let's decide who does the design.

Slide 5: A Web Design House or You?

A Web design house or you?

Slide 6: Web Design Houses

Let me tell you a bit about Web design houses. They may be graphics companies or advertising agencies that have moved into Web design. They might be new businesses that have started with the advent of the Web. They might be independent consultants and designers who are carving out a niche business in town.

The bigger firms are great for bigger businesses. They will offer slick, professional looking pages and graphics. If you want to sell a product on the Web, they will help you with e-commerce solutions and Web applications to maintain catalogues, buyer accounts, and online ordering.

However, they will probably command high fees for this work. One business owner in my town wanted to put up a small Web page for her business and was quoted a price of £3,000 for the site, promotion of the site, and maintenance by an advertising firm. In addition, she would pay for the site to be loaded on a server and a monthly fee for storage. Instead, she went through a small, independent designer, spent about £400 on design, got a great deal with a local Internet Service Provider, and still got just what she needed.

<This is a true story—use your own example or adapt this one for the presentation. The library users who attend this programme are probably more interested in the "do-it-yourself" approach, but I like starting with this to let them know there are options for higher-end Web sites.>

Slide 7: *The mime makes his decision.*

Let's say that you decide to "do-it-yourself." Here's our plan for looking at what you need to do to put together a site. Throughout these slides I may say Web site or Web pages. For our purposes in this class they are rather interchangeable.

You decide to do it yourself!

Slide 8: *Designing a Web Site*

Our plan then for designing a Web site:

I'll give you some help in getting started. We'll discuss some information design basics as well as one of the most important elements of all of this: cost considerations.

We'll then go over a plan of action that you can take with you to help organize yourself and your Web endeavours.

Finally, we'll talk about maintaining your site.

Designing a Web Site

- Getting started
- Information design basics
- Cost considerations
- Plan of action
- Maintaining your site

Slide 9: *Getting Started*

Before you do anything, do this: Look at *lots* of Web sites. Surf around the Web for sites similar to what you'd like to put up and decide what you like and don't like. You may find pages that really strike you. It's okay to look at their framework, their design, and imitate their style. That's been happening on the Web since the beginning.

Do some research as well. We'll get you started tonight by talking about site structures and basic page

Getting Started

- Look at *lots* of Web sites
- Decide what you like and don't like
- Learn about site structures
- Learn about page design and HTML

design. We'll touch on the basic elements of **HTML**, which is the name for the programming language of Web design.

<The following slides can be changed to highlight your area's local businesses and organizations. Doc Pierce's and Fischoff are used because of their local flavor for presentations I have given in Northern Indiana. I also design their pages!>

Slide 10: Web Sites: A Small Business

Here's a small business's Web site. We can learn about what works and what doesn't from looking at sites like this. What works, what doesn't? Notice they have their location and phone number right up front as well as links to various parts of their business.

This is a restaurant, so of course we'll find menus and luckily even coupons. We also get their hours and information on gift vouchers. If I needed directions, say if I were travelling to this city from somewhere else, there is a link for that as well.

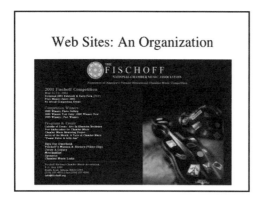

Slide 11: Web Sites: An Organization

Here's an organization's page. This is the Fischoff National Chamber Music Association front page. Look at all of the links they provide to other documents on their site. Any information I might need about participating in or attending the competition they sponsor is available off this page.

Look in the bottom left-hand corner at the contact information. That's one of my favourite parts of Web design: placing that information—where we are and how to get in touch with us—in easy-to-find locations. Don't hide your contact info from your site visitors!

Slide 12: Sample Sites?

So, how do you find pages similar to what you'd like to put up on the Web? One great resource is the Open Directory Project. Located at *www.dmoz.org*, the Open Directory Project offers pages and pages of links to Web sites organized by subject.

If you are interested in designing pages for your church, you'll find a listing of regional church sites to choose from. If you are interested in a hobbyist page, like for collecting china or antiques, try a DMOZ search.

Slide 13: Site Structures

After checking out a series of Web sites for inspiration and ideas, it's a good idea to begin considering how your Web pages or site will be constructed. Site structure refers to the way pages are arranged.

For example:

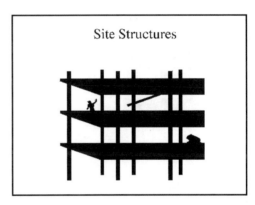

Slide 14: Tells a Story

Here's a type of design that tells a story. This linear method has pages following one after the other in order. It's great for stories or instructions that need to be followed exactly in sequence. It might also be used for creating training on the Web, where each slide is part of a lesson.

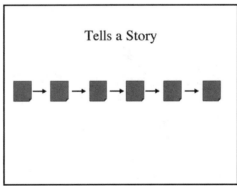

Slide 15: Hierarchy

The hierarchy is different. A main page leads surfers to other pages. The main page may contain an introduction to what the pages below it will present with more depth.

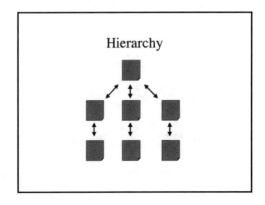

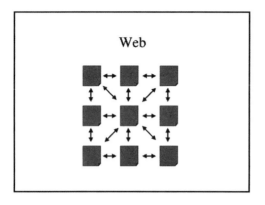

Slide 16: Web

Here's the Web format—all of the pages are linked together. You do not need to follow any linear plan for accessing the information. This is a popular format for many Web pages. One of these documents may be the start page or homepage but all of them are linked together. However, a more useful design and one we see most often—

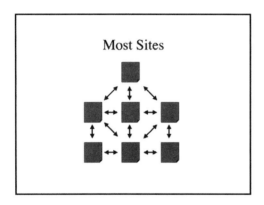

Slide 17: Most Sites

—is a hybrid of the Web and hierarchy designs. Note the main page is prominent and everything stems from it but all of the pages are still connected. I might use this design to create my own personal Web pages like this:

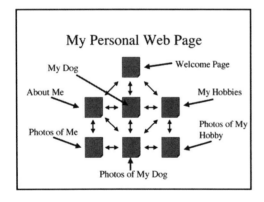

Slide 18: My Personal Web Page

Here I have a main page and then links off it to information about my dog, my hobbies, and me. Each of those pages has links to the others as well as links to photo galleries for each of my interests. This is a typical plan for a personal Web site. You may want to copy it for your own. This slide is reproduced in your handout.

Slide 19: My Business Web Page

And this same design can easily be used for your small business. Here, instead of pictures of my dog, we find information on clients, products, and our company's history.

Slide 20: My Organization Web Page

One more, okay? Here's an organization—maybe a museum or a church or an association like Fischoff. It still fits into this layout.

Of course, this is a very simple example, and many Web sites will be much more complex, with more levels and pages.

Can you see this layout as a starting point for your design? What sections might you include?

<Allow audience to respond.>

My Organization Web Page

Our Goals — Welcome Page
About Us — Our Programme
Officer Biographies — Calendar
Our Mission

Slide 21: Design Considerations

In all of these formats for layout there are some things to keep in mind. Design considerations are important from the outset because they help structure your pages and provide stability and user-friendliness. For example, consider navigation. Is it easy to move around your pages? Have you provided links back to the homepage or starting point as well as links to other sections. Are you stranding surfers on a page where the only way out is using the browser's back button?

Usability is a hot topic in the Web design world as well as in libraries. Librarians are very conscious of how easy it is to access and locate information on Web sites. Library pages—like ours at *<your library URL here>*—are created with the user in mind. Are we making it hard for surfers to find certain pages or bits of information? We might finish our page and know exactly how to navigate it—where to click, and so forth. A surfer might come in and not intuitively understand how to move around. This is an important consideration. I urge you to read up in Web design books or on the Web itself for more on this topic. Your handout has some URLs to visit devoted to this topic.

Consistency is also important. A site where every page has different navigation buttons and varying colors can be off-putting. A consistent look and feel, even within each section, allows users to navigate each new part of the site without stopping to learn how the page is set up.

Design Considerations

- Navigation - Is it easy to move around?
- Usability - Can Web surfers access all pages?
- Consistency - Do the pages have a theme?

Links

- The basis of the WWW
- Do your links work?
- Do I need permission to link to a site?

Slide 22: Links

Links are the basis of the World Wide Web; without them it's just a fancy slide projector. You'll have links on your pages between your different documents, like a link on the "My Dog" page to the "Pictures of My Dog" page.

You'll probably also have external links. External links go out onto the Web to other documents on other servers. I may want to have links on my organization's page out to other similar organizations or groups with an affiliation to my group. You may want to ask that group to link to you as well. That's one of the greatest things about the Web. A link is a free pathway to more information, further expansion on a topic, or a gateway to even more resources.

When creating your pages and for as long as your site exists, make sure your links work. Check them and recheck them. I am amazed at the fluid nature of the Web sometimes. Sites move or go down with little notice.

You might be wondering now—do we need permission to link to a site? Probably not—it's rather like a compliment to have someone link to you or vice versa. If in doubt, an e-mail requesting permission to link, and to let the other site know you might like a return link, is perfectly appropriate.

Some commercial sites do request that you link to their home page, rather than any of the other pages on their site. There are various reasons for this: some of their pages may change at short notice, or there may be commercial implications in linking to certain pages. If in doubt, ask.

Questions?

<Allow audience to respond.>

Slide 23: Learning HTML

Your next goal is to learn the basics of HTML, which stands for **Hypertext Markup Language.**

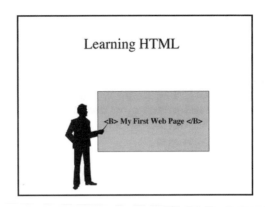

Slide 24: Basic HTML

Scary sounding name, isn't it? I promise you, it's not that bad. HTML is simply a programming language that tells a Web browser how to display a text document a certain way. Just like word processing, you key in a series of codes that are "read" by the browser and turned into the beautiful, colourful pages we see while surfing.

We could spend days with the commands involved in HTML. We could enroll in a class and spend weeks learning the coding. But for this class, I want to give you a basic understanding of what it's like to work in HTML inside the broader goal of the session—to get you on your way to designing and implementing a Web site for your hobby, small business, or organization.

Simply put, then, HTML involves using brackets to surround design commands. That is the whole basis for the language: marking up a text document to control the way sentences, characters, or design elements look when viewed in a Web browser.

Commands in HTML are called **tags.** For example, the tag to make text bold is a letter B. Brackets open a command like this bracket-letter B-bracket combination and then a bracket-slash B-bracket closes the command. This will make the text appear in bold on the page.

Sample HTML Tags

- Bold <B>
- Italics <I>
- Center <CENTER>
- Heading Sizes <H1> <H2> etc.
- Paragraph <P>
- Blink <BLINK>

Slide 25: Sample HTML Tags

Here are some basic style tags in HTML. These are used to format the way text appears on your page. It's very similar to word processing. Notice that we can format text to be bold, as we discussed, and in italics as well.

We can also change the size of headings in our pages. These headings sizes, "Heading 1," "Heading 2," and so on, correspond to a certain size of type on the page. "Heading 1" is the largest. "Heading 6" is the smallest.

The paragraph tag allows us to insert line breaks. You have to do that in HTML or the lines would run on and on.

Here's a quirky one: the blink command. That command causes text to blink on your page. You might see the word "new" or "updated" flashing on someone's page. That's what the blink tag does. Let me say this about the blink command: A little blinking on your page goes a long, long way. Use it sparingly! In fact, some of the resources listed in your handouts that detail what not to do on your pages advise never to use the blink command.

Basic HTML

My Home Page

Welcome to my home page on the WWW!

Slide 26: Basic HTML

Here's our friend again. He's made his first page. It's very simple with a large heading, a horizontal divider line, and some text.

Slide 27: Basic HTML

Here is the HTML coding that makes it look the way it does. Here you can see the basic framework of a Web page. All pages will have this framework.

<Here you may want to point to each element with a pointer or your hand.>

We begin with an open HTML command.

Then we open the HEAD area of the page. In this area is the title of the page that shows up at the top of the browser window. Note that you cannot really format the text of this area. It can't be bold or italic. It just displays as the title of the window. Watch for this when you surf.

In the HEAD area we insert a TITLE tag and then close the TITLE and close the HEAD tags. See the slashes closing those commands?

Then we open the BODY of the document. This is where the full content of Web pages go between the open and close BODY commands.

Here in our example our friend has inserted a heading for the page and made it size 1. Notice the heading command is closed at the end of the line. This text is also centreed using the open and closed CENTER command. After that we have a <HR>, which inserts a horizontal rule across the page.

Then we have our text—the body of the page, including the PARAGRAPH tag that inserts a line break or carriage return in the page. This example has just one line of text; other pages may be longer.

Finally, in all HTML pages we close the BODY tag and close the tag we began with, the HTML tag.

Seems rather simple, doesn't it? The basic framework is very simple, but Web pages can become very intricate and detailed. I wanted you to get an idea, however, of what the basic building blocks are.

Basic HTML

```
<HTML>
<HEAD><TITLE>My Corner of the Web</TITLE>
</HEAD><BODY>
<CENTER><H1>My Home Page</H1></CENTER><HR>
<P>Welcome to my home page on the WWW!
</BODY>
</HTML>
```

Page Editors Make It Easy

- Application programs
  - Microsoft FrontPage
  - Adobe PageMill
  - Macromedia Dreamweaver
- Save as Web page
- Common interfaces

Slide 28: Page Editors Make It Easy

It gets even easier to design Web pages if you use page-editing software. There are programs like Microsoft FrontPage or Adobe PageMill that create pages using a graphical interface. Just like MS Word or PageMaker, these software programs allow you to do the design with menu options and formatting selections. These programs are also referred to as "authoring tools."

Programs you own now, such as Word or other word-processing applications, probably have a "Save As Web Page" selection. You might want to read up on it in your software manuals.

One nice thing about design software or using programs you own is the common interfaces found in many packages, like Microsoft products. If you have mastered Word, you'll probably be pretty comfortable with FrontPage.

Advanced Applications

- Adobe PhotoShop
- Adobe ImageReady
- Macromedia Flash
- XML

Slide 29: Advanced Applications

I'd like to mention just a few of the higher-end applications that help Web designers make flashy pages. These programs are rather costly and require some experience and training, but they are very popular in the design community.

PhotoShop has been around a long time. It is a professional-grade image manipulation program. A Web designer might use this program to augment and edit images for Web sites. ImageReady is a counterpart to PhotoShop that optimizes Web images for retrieval.

Flash creates animations and helps make pages interactive. You may visit pages devoted to new movies or entertainment endeavors. These sites probably incorporate Flash effects in some way.

XML takes HTML a step farther. It allows you to create your own markup language to create your own pages.

I don't want to overwhelm you, and for now do not worry about these programs. If you are interested in any of these advanced applications, the library has books on many of these subjects.

How are we doing? Questions?

<Allow audience to respond.>

Slide 30: Cost Considerations

Okay, let's talk about cost. We've looked at site structure and simple HTML. We've discussed applications that will help us. What might all of this cost?

Cost Considerations

£

Slide 31: Costs include:

Here's a breakdown of what you might expect to pay for if you are putting up a Web site. These include: Web page design fees if you have a designer work for you, domain name costs which we'll discuss in a moment, hosting costs for that domain, monthly dial-up access if you need it, and other miscellaneous expenses. The other expenses might include promotional costs, supplies, and costs associated with images.

Costs include:

- Web page design fees (if any)
- Domain name costs
- Domain hosting costs
- Monthly dial-up (if needed)
- Other miscellaneous expenses

Slide 32: Do you buy a Domain Name?

So, do you buy a domain name? A domain name is that address we see for many businesses and organizations.

Take a look at these examples. Remember from the *Introduction to the Internet* class that a .com signifies a business and a .org signifies an organization. The .net extension applies to many businesses that have a connection to the Internet or computer technology.

There are new domains available now as well. Just approved are .biz, .info, .museum, .aero, .pro, .coop, and .name. Of those, .biz and .info are available for purchase through sites like Network Solutions. Domains with the new ending .museum are reserved for museums and are called "chartered" domains on the Network Solutions page.

That does not mean all of the .coms have been purchased. A creative name can still be registered with an ending of .com.

Do you buy a Domain Name?

- www.yourbusiness.com
- www.yourorganization.org
- www.yourinternetrelatedbusiness.net
- New domains on the way!

Domain Names

- £10 a year from a registration company
- Register online easily

www.mimeforhire.com

Slide 33: Domain Names

How do you get a domain name? You can register with a name company online and actually do the whole process from your computer. It's also one of the best values on the Web—about £10 a year.

There are some Web companies that will register your domain for free and host it, but they usually put up banner ads at the top and bottom of your pages. This may work for some endeavors, but not all. Take a look at *www.namezero.com* to see how one of these sites works.

Ponder what domain you might like to have. Is it still available? How can you check? A Web site like Network Solutions at *www.networksolutions* has a search box at the top of the page to check and see if a name is still available.

Have you heard about the people who buy domains like johntesh.com or barbarawalters.com and then try to sell them to the highest bidder? Domains are big business. They also get wrapped up in litigation sometimes! John Tesh (an American musician) sued to get his name back from the person who registered it.

<I have checked my name and someone has bought www.michaelstephens.com. *Phil Bradley owns* www. philb.com, *but someone else registered* www. philbradley.com. *You might check your name and tell the class about your findings.>*

Has anyone here bought a domain name? What did you buy?

<Allow audience to respond. Discuss a bit if possible.>

Web Site Hosting

- ISPs charge £10 to £100 a month for hosting
- Depends on the level of service and traffic
- Shop around!

Slide 34: Web Site Hosting

Web hosting is the final step of your creation process. Your HTML files are uploaded using the **File Transfer Protocol** or **FTP** to a server for storage. That server is accessible to the Web so anyone with a connection and a browser can view it.

For Web site hosting with an Internet Service Provider, expect to pay from £10 to £100 a month, depending on the level of service you require. E-commerce sites where you may be taking orders and selling products will cost more. Traffic to your site can play into the numbers as well. High-traffic sites may have to pay a bit more for all of the bandwidth they are using.

Here's an important tip: Shop around for the best value and best deal for what you need to get a site on the Web. Some ISPs will give you a few meg of space automatically. Maybe that's all you need. If you need a domain name, though, expect to pay a bit more for that added service.

Take a look in the phone book under Internet providers and make some calls. Use the handouts and your notes from this class as well to ask about certain types of hosting and domains. You will also find pricing information on most ISP Web sites.

Slide 35: Here's Our Plan

Here's our plan of action then. Follow these steps to success in designing and putting up your pages.

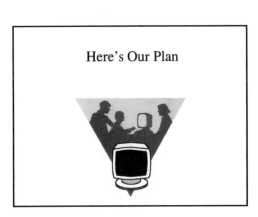

Slide 36: Action Plan for Site Design

Some of these things we've covered but here is the step-by-step process.

Start by planning your page layout structure and assemble your sources for content. Then organize your content into the layout and mess with it! Move it around on paper or on index cards until you get a structure you like. Remember navigation and usability too!

Then input your text into your favourite word processor and assemble the pages in HTML or in a page editor like Microsoft FrontPage. Add your images and links. Finally, upload your pages to your server or ISP and then promote your pages to get the word out.

Action Plan for Site Design

- Plan your site layout
- Gather your resources for content
- Organize content into layout
- Input your text
- Add images and links as needed
- Place pages on a server
- Promote your pages

Invaluable Resources

• Tips for Web design in class handouts
• Books available at the library
• Search the Web for more!

Slide 37: Invaluable Resources

You will always have help along the way. Talk to friends and associates who have done Web work or have pages up. Remember, too, the invaluable resources of the library and on the Web. There are some URLs in the handouts for you to look at as well.

Content Counts!

Slide 38: Content Counts!

I haven't said too much about it yet—but content counts!

Content

• Most pages or sites include:
   – Your message
   – Contact information
   – Table of contents
   – FAQs
   – Biographies

Slide 39: Content

When you surf around the Web, you'll find that most pages or sites include many of the same elements. Your pages will probably be the same. Think about your goals for your own Web site as we look at these.

Include your message—what you want to say. It might be information about your business, organization, or personal interest. This is the most important part of your site.

Include your contact information. For businesses, that should be address, phone, fax, and e-mail. It's frustrating to find a business page that hides or doesn't even include a way to get in touch. For organizations, the same applies; give as much contact info as you'd like. For personal use pages—my collection or my dog or whatever—you may only need to include an e-mail address.

A table of contents gives users an idea of what is included on your page and an FAQ answers those questions you feel most of your users may want to know about.

You may want to include biographies of key personnel in your business or organization as well as your personal biography if you feel comfortable putting it on the Web.

Slide 40: Content Considerations

Here are some other points to consider when you develop your content.

Who is your audience? Decide who you want to appeal to or who you want to visit your site. Create your content for them: your customers, your supporters, your congregation, or persons with a similar interest.

Put the most important part of your content at the top of pages or where it can be easily found. Don't hide your information under layers of fluff or graphics.

Remember to proofread all of your text. It does not look good for a business or organization to have typos on their pages. Personal pages too can suffer from mistakes in spelling and grammar.

A huge page of text that takes awhile to load on a home connection may turn people off. If possible, have something appear on the screen within 15 seconds—preferably less. They may not wait for the whole page to load or they may click back and exit your site. If you have a lot of text, try dividing it into sections and separate pages.

Finally, and this is part of maintaining your pages, update often. If your content appears old or dated, surfers will not stay around. Give them reasons to come back, like "Check in soon for our new product line," or "Return next month for a look at our organization's plans for 2003."

How are we doing? Questions?

<Allow audience to respond.>

Content Considerations

- Know your audience
- Put important information up front
- Proofread all of your text
- Watch out for LONG pages
- Update often

Slide 41: Adding Images

Now let's talk about adding images and graphics to your site.

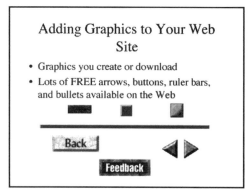

Slide 42: Adding Graphics to Your Web Site

You can spruce up your pages with neat graphics like buttons and bars and rulers to separate sections.

You might, if artistically inclined, create the graphics yourself in a paint or image program. That way you can have exactly what you want for your pages.

This slide, however, has a sampling of graphics downloaded from various sites on the Web. These were all available free and with no copyright. Sometimes a designer will put up graphics and just ask if you use them to link to the page they came from.

There are probably hundreds of choices available on the Web as well as those graphics libraries you can purchase or those that come with your Web page design software.

Slide 43: Adding Images to Your Web Site

How do you add photos to your pages? You might use a scanner and photos you have taken. Or have a photo CD or floppy made when you turn in a roll of pictures you have taken for the site. Many larger stores that do developing offer these services, as do the Web sites that have sprung up that store photos. You send them your film which they develop and post on the Web.

You might also have a digital camera. That is an invaluable tool if you are creating a site that will rely on lots of images of products or items in a collection. If you are an estate agent, you may want to take digital photos of a property to post on the Web to help sell it.

Here's a sunflower caught with a digital camera in a

summer garden. This might be a nice addition to a personal Web page on gardening. It's amazing how versatile the digital camera can be.

<Don't hesitate to do a plug for the digital camera module if you plan on presenting it in the near future.>

Slide 44: Image Formats

We should mention image formats here. The two most prevalent types of image files on the Web are **GIF** files and **JPEG** files. Some people say "jiff" and some people say "gif." But it means **Graphic Interchange Format**, one of the first means of transferring images on the Internet, developed by CompuServe over ten years ago.

JPEG is short for **Joint Photographic Experts Group**, and it can reduce files sizes for efficient use with Web pages.

GIFs are best for logos and graphics—like the buttons and rulers we saw on the earlier slide. JPEG files are best for photos. In fact, most digital cameras shoot in JPEG mode.

Here's a nice picture of Snoqualmie Falls in Washington state, saved as a JPEG and ready for a Web site. I might have taken a holiday in Washington and photographed all sorts of scenery. I may be putting up a "My Trip to Seattle" page. In JPEG mode, the photos are ready to be added to the pages and uploaded.

Image Formats

- GIF: Graphic Interchange Format
  - Best for logos and graphics
- JPEG
  - Best for pictures

Slide 45: Image Considerations

Here's a bit more to think about when using images on your pages.

The size of an image file can be anywhere from a few kilobytes to a megabyte. Remember, though, that Web surfers might be coming to your site with a slower connection. Many will not wait for a huge graphic file to load. Optimize your images with whatever graphics program you have. Earlier we mentioned Adobe PhotoShop. There are other less expensive but powerful graphic programs out there. Usually if you buy a scanner or digital camera, you'll get some software too.

Image Considerations

- Watch out for large graphic files
- Don't use copyrighted images

Don't use copyrighted images on your pages unless you get permission or own the copyright. Some copyright holders will get in touch with you and ask you to cease and desist if you are using their images. Fox TV did that with *The Simpsons* a few years ago when they cracked down on sites using images of the animated family. Since then they have recognized the importance of fan pages on the Web and just ask that if you use *Simpsons* or *X-Files* images cite their source and add a text disclaimer to your pages.

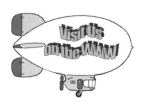

Slide 46: Promoting Your Pages

All right, you've done the work. You've mastered page design. You've shot some pictures. You've uploaded to your ISP's server. The next step is promoting your work.

Slide 47: Promoting Your Pages

Here's a checklist of things to do to make sure the word gets out about your new site.

Put your new URL on all cards and correspondence. Make it a part of every piece of advertising you do: newspaper ads, fliers, and posters. If your organization is having a meeting, make an announcement and put the address on a leaflet.

Announce it on appropriate sites or e-mail lists. If you've done a page about your dog, post the URL to a list or newsgroup devoted to that breed. If you've completed extensive work on your chinaware collector's site, announce at all the chinaware-themed lists and Web sites you can find. Do not, however, **spam** multiple lists. Spamming is where one indiscriminately sends a message to as many recipients as possible, regardless of interest or appropriateness.

Submit your URL to search engines. Do not pay someone to do this. You can do it yourself at most search sites. Some have started charging for a listing. You need to decide if it's worth it to pay.

One businessperson putting up a page was told that for an additional $500 the Web design company would make sure all of the search engines indexed the site. Don't do it unless you have a lot of cash for the project—many Web search sites will allow you to manually submit a URL.

Finally, write quality **metatags**.

Slide 48: Metatags

What are metatags? They are descriptors that are hidden on your pages inside the HTML programming in the HEAD area. Metatags describe your pages with invisible keywords.

Who reads the tags? We can't see them on a page, but who can?

\<Allow audience to respond.\>

Right—the search engines. That's what can see those invisible keywords on the page. You might remember from earlier classes that the search engines send out automated spiders to index Web pages. The spiders look at words on pages and build the index that we can search. So invisible keywords help establish our rankings at the different search engines.

Slide 49: Castle in the Country Web Site

Here's a nice page for a bed-and-breakfast in Michigan. Good design. They are following many of our guidelines for design: information about the establishment, rates, directions, and even some virtual tours. But let's take a look at what is happening behind the scenes with their metatagging.

```
<html>
<head>
<title>Castle in the Country Bed and Breakfast</title>
<META name="description" content="Bed and Breakfast Inns of Michigan.">
<META name="keywords" content="bed breakfast, michigan, MI,
bed and breakfast, bandb, inn, inns, accommodations, lodging, travel,
country inns, hotels, motels, retreats, tourism, guide, directory, USA,
United States, fishing, golf, tennis, biking, skiing, hiking,
children, pets, national park, AAA, romantic, intimate,
getaway, romantic, relaxing, vegetarian, smoking, antiques, beach,
horseback riding, Jacuzzi, shopping, restaurant, tavern, bar,
historic, Allegan, Jones, Kalamazoo, Mendon, New Buffalo,
Saugatuck, South Haven, St Joseph, Union Pier, lakeshore,
amish michigan">
```

Castle in the Country's Metatagging

Slide 50: Viewing Source for Castle in the Country

Here is a bit of the HTML coding for the Castle in the Country Web site. Look at the metatags. There is a description field: "Bed & Breakfast Inns of Michigan." Then there are the keywords. The keywords include the names of towns in that area of Michigan, activities you might find at the B&B as well as nearby, and other keywords. The HTML programmer hopes that people searching for a place to stay in Michigan will find this one.

To go a step farther, if we did a search for "vegetarian Jacuzzi shopping" we would probably find this site in the results because all of those words are in the tagging.

Questions?

Maintaining Your Site

Slide 51: Maintaining Your Site

We are almost at the end. So much information! Please remember your handouts. Last up, is maintaining your site.

Maintaining Your Site

- Update often and date pages
- Keep content fresh and interesting
- Give reasons for visitors to return
- Check links and images
- Devote time

Slide 52: Maintaining Your Site

Here is our final checklist. Things to do to maintain your site after you've put it up.

Update your pages often. Date each page as well. You might input at the bottom of the page: "Created on January 3, 2001, Updated March 16, 2001." That lets visitors know when the page was put up and when it was last updated.

Some surfers may not be interested in your message if the page is dated 1997 or if the information itself seems out-of-date.

So when you are updating your site, keep the content fresh and interesting. Promote what's new in your business. Highlight your organization's current activities season to season or month to month.

Give reasons for visitors to return to your pages. That's what updating is all about. Keep them interested in your site.

Check your links and images often to make sure they work. Links to external pages can easily change. Check them or buy software that checks them for you if you have a lot to do.

Images might not have been linked correctly at the outset or might have been updated in such a way that they no longer work. It's frustrating for a visitor to find that broken image icon instead of the picture they hoped to see and you wanted to show them.

Finally, devote the time needed to do all of these things. Maintaining a Web site can be almost a full-time job for some businesses or groups. In the library world, having a site requires a lot of staff time for upkeep. You may find that as well, as you delve into creating pages.

Slide 53: Thanks!

Thank you! We have covered a lot of detailed material in this class. Are there comments or questions?

Module 8
Exploring Internet
Video and Audio

INTRODUCTION

As your users discover more and more about the content and power of the Internet, they may be ready to experiment with downloading or streaming video or audio files. How many offices in your library already have staff that tune in to Web radio stations for workday music?

The idea of multimedia content delivered to a PC can be mystifying. This module will demystify some of the most popular formats and provide an in-depth look at MP3 files. A final section describes the steps taken in ripping and burning CDRs, a procedure that has become popular as the prices of CD recorders and blanks have fallen.

WORKSHOP ATTENDEES WILL GAIN:

1. An understanding of downloading multimedia on the Internet.
2. An overview of what types of video and audio can be found on the Web.
3. A discussion and definition of MP3 and peer-to-peer computing.
4. A look at how CDs can be created from music files downloaded from the Web.

TIPS FOR PRESENTING THIS MODULE

- The clip of Snoqualmie Falls in Snoqualmie, Washington, is included in the presentation and on the CD-ROM. Use your own movie files for this presentation if you'd like. Download a trailer from a current popular movie or other fun clip. For classes in 1997 and 1998 when the movie *Titanic* was a hot topic, I demonstrated clips of a computer-generated *Titanic* sailing through icy seas.

- Use a PC with good speakers and some MP3 files to demonstrate how good an MP3 can sound. Favourites I have used: "California Dreamin'" by The Mamas and the Papas or any Fleetwood Mac tune that hopefully will appeal to all age groups. Maybe have music playing before the class starts.
- Stress copyright implications and do not advocate song piracy, acknowledge that people do make CDs for their own personal use even though it is not permitted under the copyright law in the UK.
- Update this module each time you present it. What's the new, hot, cutting-edge thing on the Web in the multimedia arena? Include it!

MODULE 8—EXPLORING INTERNET VIDEO AND AUDIO—SCRIPT

Slide 1: Introduction

<Introduce yourself and your helper if you have one. Tell the group that you will be using a presentation program called PowerPoint to present the programme.>

Slide 2: Our Goals

Welcome to the class on exploring Internet video and audio. Here are our goals for this session. We'll discuss our topics and pay special attention to MP3 technology and making your own CDs. Then we'll talk about the future of multimedia on the Internet.

I'll use terms like multimedia or clip to describe the video or audio content we can find on the Internet.

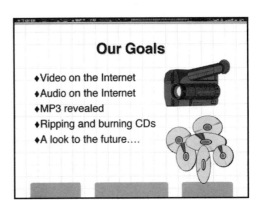

Slide 3: Download Methods

First we need to look at how we get multimedia—video and audio—off the Internet. There are two ways to download. One is to download the entire clip, then play it with software on your computer. The other is to play the clip as it downloads and that's known as **streaming**. To stream a file your PC must be connected to the Internet.

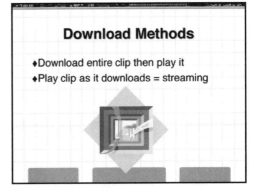

Slide 4: Downloading Clips

When you download a multimedia file it might take a while, especially if you are at home with a 56k connection. At home, though, you might start a 6-meg download and have time to go make a sandwich and let the dog out and get back in time to see it finish. At work or at school, with faster connections, a movie file or song clip might zip down much faster.

When the clip is down, you open it using a piece of software already installed on your computer: a video player or an audio player.

Slide 5: Streaming Media

Streaming media is a different kind of download. The browser or application that you are using begins to display or play without downloading the entire clip. You are able to see the movie clip start or hear the first few seconds of the song. Streaming files work well with faster connections.

You can stream on a 56k line, but if you have a cable modem or an ADSL connection or network connection, the streams can play at real time. We can watch the movie clip with few snags or skips or hear a song without any skips or loss of quality. A **buffer** in streaming media acts to pull in a few seconds extra before the clip starts so breaks are reduced once the clip begins to play.

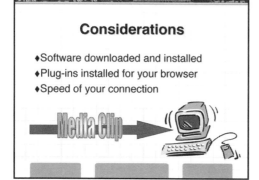

Slide 6: Considerations

There are several considerations for dealing with multimedia and the Internet. You need to have the right software downloaded, installed, and functional on your computer. If media is coming in to your Web browser, such as Netscape or Microsoft Internet Explorer, you may need certain **plug-ins** installed for your browser to display the media correctly.

The speed of your connection is very important. I would not attempt too much streaming or downloading of larger files with a connection below 28.8. At

28.8 you'd have to wait a long time for results and it might be rather frustrating.

Are there any questions about the basics of getting multimedia on the Internet?

<Allow audience to respond.>

Slide 7: Popular Players

Popular software to play media includes the ones listed here. Take a look at these URLs next time you are on the Internet. You can download software at each of them. The Windows Media Player is probably already on your PC if you have a recent version of Windows.

Slide 8: Video on the Internet

Let's take a look at what kind of video you'll find on the Internet.

Slide 9: What will we find?

What kind of clips will we find? Here's a list of some of the content we'll find.

Movie trailers or promotions for upcoming movies are a lot of fun. Movie studios like to make clips available as a promotional tool, usually for the next hot new movie. They will probably post clips on their sites in a variety of download speeds or in streaming format.

Independent Web productions are little movies made especially for the Web. They might be comedy shorts,

spoofs of movies like *The Blair Witch Project*, ongoing soap opera-style stories, and more. Some content has a huge following, like certain animated "shows" found only on the Web.

Educational clips abound on the Web, from short clips detailing how the *Titanic* sank, to video of scientific endeavours from NASA. Children might find it especially useful to look at clips that come from the NASA pages or other scientific agencies.

Entertainment and news are very popular on the Web. A site like the BBC will offer video of breaking stories daily. These sites sometimes archive video from big stories, so if you are researching a topic you can look back and see how it was covered.

Slide 10: Video Content URLs

Here are URLs for some of the content you might be looking for. Remember that you can use Google or the Open Directory Project (DMOZ) to search for any other content you might be interested in, such as independent film, Web cartoons, or soap operas.

Slide 11: Video on the Internet

Most video clips on the Internet will be in one of these **formats** or **file types**: QuickTime™ clips, MPEG movies, or RealVideo™. Let's look at each of these.

Slide 12: QuickTime™

QuickTime™, developed by Apple™ Computer, enhances many of its Macintosh applications. It can play video clips and animations and display still formats. This system will work on Macs and PCs, but the PC must have the QuickTime™ driver installed on the machine to work correctly.

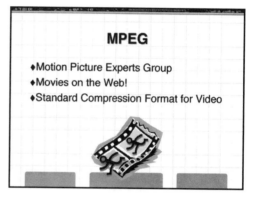

Slide 13: MPEG

MPEG movies are a standard on the Internet, developed by the same people that developed the **JPEG** format for images. The Motion Picture Experts Group got together and developed a standard for delivering motion clips or movies on the Web. MPEG is a standard compression format for video. You may see a movie file that ends with .mpg—that's an MPEG file.

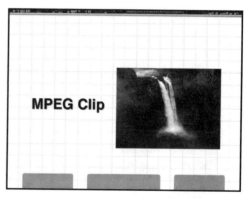

Slide 14: MPEG Clip

Here is an MPEG clip of lovely Snoqualmie Falls in Washington state. It was taken with a digital camera that captures MPEG-format movies and plays them back with the QuickTime™ system. Let's take a look.

<Click on movie. Let it play. Or change this and play the short clip you created.>

I might have found that movie on the Web and wanted to see what the falls look like. Downloading it, I could watch it and possibly save it to my hard drive if I wanted to keep it.

Slide 15: RealVideo™ Format

RealVideo™ format was developed by the people at RealNetworks to stream video content from various servers with easy-to-manage file sizes. Take a look at their Web site to download their proprietary software, the RealPlayer, and scan all of the content choices. You'll find news, interviews, music videos, and more.

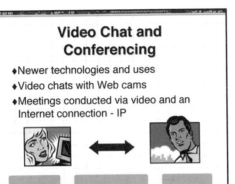

Slide 16: Video Chat and Conferencing

Let's discuss video chat and conferencing. These are newer technologies.

Video chats with Web cams have been around for a while, but faster connections allow them to be virtually in real time. Trudy here might connect to Tom's computer—both of them armed with a small Web cam device—and carry out a chat complete with picture and sound. Visit your favourite electronics store to see how many types of Web cam devices there are on the market.

Video conferencing is probably a little more serious activity than chatting. Meetings conducted using video conferencing software on camera-equipped PCs via an Internet connection are not uncommon these days. A national company, for example, may meet once a month for a video staff meeting, with participants checking in from all over the country. The meeting takes place in real time, as if in one large conference room.

This format is also well-suited to academic endeavours such as distance learning programmes at schools, colleges, and universities.

Slide 17: Digital Video Revolution

Another aspect of multimedia, and especially video on the Web, is the **digital video** revolution taking place as our newer PCs and Macs come out with **DV** features. DV cams, short for digital video cameras, have made it possible to connect your camera to a PC or Mac and pull in video footage as digital data.

These computers function as digital video editors with professional features once available only to those in high-end production houses. Now, anyone with the right equipment can title a video, include transitions, use fades, change scenes with dissolves, and more.

Slide 18: Digital Video Revolution

You can also add music and sound effects to your own creations and output the finished movie to your VCR. Imagine the family reunion video with all types of effects, titles like "Grandma Runs the Sack Race," and a professional crawl of credits at the end.

A movie made by me!

The possibilities for the future of home DV editing and uploading to the Web seem huge. We'll be able to share movies instead of pictures as connection speeds get faster and faster.

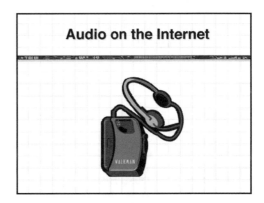

Slide 19: Audio on the Internet

Now, let's look at audio on the Internet.

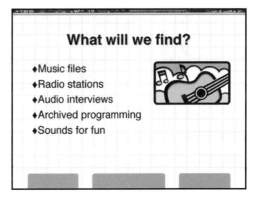

Slide 20: What will we find?

What will we discover when we encounter audio on the Internet? We'll find music files or clips, radio stations playing all sorts of music, audio interviews with notable personalities, archived programming that we might have missed the first time around, and sounds for fun.

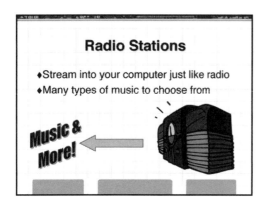

Slide 21: Radio Stations

Radio stations stream music into your computer just like real "off the air" radio. There are many types of music to choose from: classic rock, classical, progressive rock, adult contemporary, and more. Many larger radio stations have a Web streaming component so people in other parts of the country can listen as well.

Other stations exist solely on the Web for Web listeners to enjoy on their computers.

Slide 22: Archived Programming

Archived clips are found on the Web as well. The BBC Radio site is a perfect example. This site provides live links to its radio stations and also has some archived programmes as well.

Other sites archive audio clips of interviews or songs as well. Next time you're surfing, look for sites that feature audio content and try them out.

Slide 23: Internet Audio

Here are some of the other types of Internet audio.

Remember I mentioned fun sounds? Many of those will be in the .wav file format. A file called vaderdad.wav might be Darth Vader from *Star Wars* saying "Luke, I am your father." These files are used on your PC to enhance some actions with sound, like ejecting a disk or announcing an e-mail has been received. The computer voice from *2001: A Space Odyssey* is downloaded a lot to make a computer "speak."

RealAudio™ is the companion to RealVideo™. Sound clips stream into your computer from various sources and play with the RealPlayer software. Again, these might be clips of a song or an interview with some notable person. Many music store sites offer Real clips of songs on CDs to sample while you browse.

Liquid Audio is another format of music delivery developed by the Liquid Audio company, a format that seeks to solve some of the legal and copyright issues involved with exchanging music over the Net. The format lets you listen to music with high sound quality using the Liquid Music Player. You can purchase the songs that you like in their format to download onto your PC. Liquid Audio tracks can be played on your PC sound system or recorded to CDR disk.

Then we come to MP3 format, one of the most popular and notable formats for audio on the Internet. Let's take a look.

Slide 24: MP3 Revealed

And now . . . MP3 revealed!

Slide 25: What is MP3?

What is MP3? It's the file extension for MPEG, audio layer 3. That's a techie way of saying that MP3 is part of the MPEG system, specifically audio, that shrinks the original sound data from a CD without losing sound quality.

A CD track in its normal form might be 40 megabytes for a 4 minute song. An MP3 file for that same song might be four meg. Because they are rather small, MP3 files can easily be downloaded and uploaded on the Internet.

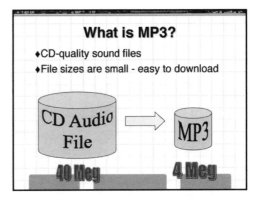

Slide 26: Peer-to-Peer Computing

Have you heard of **Napster** or **Gnutella**? They are applications that support **peer-to-peer computing**. That means that through a system like Napster, I can connect directly to another Napster user's hard drive and download files from his MP3 directory.

Napster or Gnutella allows users to search for a certain song, locate it on any number of other users' computers, and download it.

Controversy arises when copyrighted songs are distributed this way. I might find a hot new song with Napster, download, and not have to buy the CD it's on. It's a format embroiled in litigation and copyright issues. We could spend our entire time together discussing it.

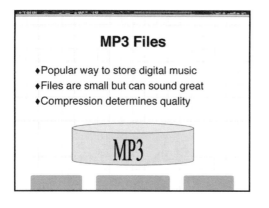

Slide 27: MP3 Files

For personal use, however, MP3 files are a popular way to store digital music. Remember that the files are small but can sound great. An MP3 file is created by pulling digital data off a CD with a certain amount of compression. That rate of compression determines the quality of the song.

Slide 28: MP3 Software

MP3 software programs play your songs on your PC. If you have good speakers attached to your computer, MP3 can provide some great sounding music. Some programs even catalogue your songs and create MP3 files from CD.

Slide 29: Ripping

When you compress a file from CD-quality tracks to MP3, that's called "ripping." Have you heard that term before? Have you heard young people in your life say they have been ripping CDs? That's what they mean. They are using software to create MP3s.

Slide 30: Popular Software

Here's some of the popular software that plays MP3 files. We've seen some of these before. A newer program from Apple™ is iTunes, a powerful playing and cataloguing program.

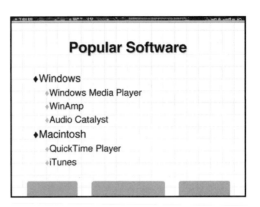

Slide 31: MP3 Players

MP3 players are devices like portable CD players that take your MP3 files with you. Usually they will have a built-in memory card where files are loaded by the software that manages your music MP3s, which are downloaded from PC to player. This type of player offers you hours of music without having to carry CDs, cassettes, or minidisks.

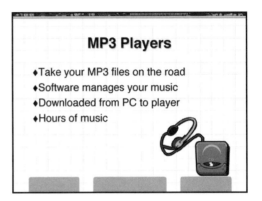

Slide 32: Popular Players

Here are some popular players on the market now.

<Update this slide as more models become available. Discuss their features here. For example, the Nomad can store so much music, the Sony product has removable media, and so forth.>

Slide 33: Burning CDs

Finally, let's talk about burning CDs. What does that mean?

<Allow audience to respond.>

Right. Creating and recording a CD.

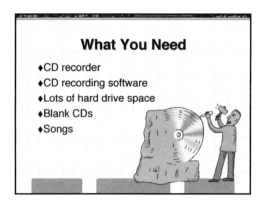

Slide 34: What You Need

If you are downloading music files or ripping your own MP3s, you may want to make your own song collections for personal use. However, make sure you copy from a legitimate website which has been endorsed by the music industry and remember, it violates copyright laws to make copies of CDs and sell them.

Here's what you need to make your own mixes and backups of favourite CDs, maybe to keep in the car.

You'll need a CD recorder and the CD recording software that probably came with the drive, lots of hard drive space because CD tracks take up a lot of room, blank CDs to record on, and the songs you want to work with.

I might want to burn all my favourite songs on one CD: _____'s Greatest Hits.

To find out what software and hardware is available to make CDs, check at your favourite electronics store or online retailer. There are many makes and models to choose from.

Slide 35: Convert MP3 Files

With your CD creation software, MP3 files are converted to CD files. CD files take up a lot more space than an MP3 as we saw before, roughly 40 meg for 4 minutes.

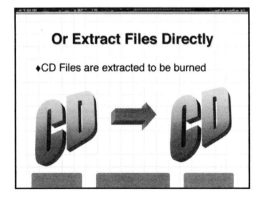

Slide 36: Or Extract Files Directly

Or you may just extract files directly from your CD collection. All of these tracks must be stored on your hard drive. Then the software lets you set the order of the songs and the length of time between songs, that's called the **pre-gap**.

Slide 37: Burning a CD

Then, you can set the recorder to do its thing: burn the CD tracks onto a blank CDR. The speed of a CD recorder varies. Some may burn at 8 times the normal playing speed, recording a 80-minute CD in 10 minutes.

You can buy fancy labels, CD case inserts, and more to make your recorded CDs look professional.

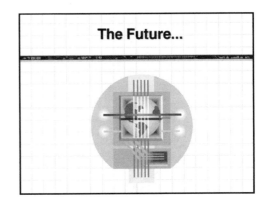

Slide 38: The Future . . .

What does the future hold for multimedia on the Internet and on our computers?

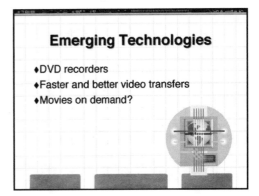

Slide 39: Emerging Technologies

Although at the moment it's not possible to burn DVD discs because the technology is too expensive for home use, this will be available in a few years, in just the same way that it took several years before CD-Recordable discs and technology became available for home use.

Faster and better video transfers will allow us to get higher quality video of news clips, chats, and conferences. Someday, we may be able to order a movie through our Internet connection and route it to our television to view! Who knows what emerging technologies will bring?

Slide 40: Thanks!

Thanks!
Questions?

Module 9
Chatting on
the Internet

INTRODUCTION

The Internet is a community. That's one of the foundations of most of the modules in the *Toolkit*. We participate. We learn. We e-mail friends and relatives, exchanging pictures. We listen to music or catch a movie trailer online. And many of us visit chat rooms.

Chatting is a popular pastime in many libraries that offer access to the Internet. It may also puzzle new users. This module explains chat and the "language of chat."

In 1998, Richard Truxall, an Internet trainer from Michigan, presented "Chatting Up a Storm" at the American Library Association national conference to a room filled with curious librarians. How would the increasingly popular chat culture affect library service? What did those terms and jargon mean? This module seeks to explain the ins and outs of chat concisely.

WORKSHOP ATTENDEES WILL GAIN:

1. An understanding of what online chat is and its many forms.
2. An examination of the jargon and symbols used in chatting.

TIPS FOR PRESENTING THIS MODULE

- Dare we offer a glimpse into an unmoderated chat room in a public class? That's a tough call. Who knows what language you may see from various chatters. If you can find a moderated chat room or create your own on one of the chat sites with a colleague to demonstrate a live chat, try it.

MODULE 9—CHATTING ON THE INTERNET—SCRIPT

Slide 1: Introduction

<Introduce yourself and your helper if you have one. Tell the group that you will be using a presentation program called PowerPoint to present the programme.>

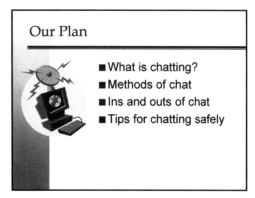

Slide 2: Our Plan

Here is our plan for the class. We'll define chatting, look at various methods of chat, and discuss some of the jargon of chatting that may seem like a foreign language. Lastly, I'll give you some tips to remember when entering the world of chat.

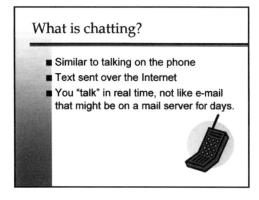

Slide 3: What is chatting?

What is chatting? In this context, it's communicating over a computer connection instead of talking directly to a person. It is similar to talking on the phone with someone, but instead of speaking you are typing and sending text over the Internet.

It's not like e-mailing someone. To chat, both parties or the whole group must be connected to the Internet and in a chat program or chat Web site at the same time. E-mail might wait on a mail server for days before someone reads it. Chat is instantaneous.

Slide 4: Types of Chat

There are different ways to chat on the Internet. We access these forms of chat in various ways from downloading the software we need to chat to simply accessing a Web site and logging in to a Web chat room. Let's take a look at each of these methods. Some you may be familiar with and some may be new to you.

Types of Chat

- Text-based
- Web-based
- Instant messaging
- Emerging methods

Slide 5: Text-Based Chat

The most basic and oldest type of Internet chat is text-based chat. Using this method involves either accessing a chat room via a telnet connection or downloading a special program that connects to chat servers.

The most prominent text-based chat uses the Internet Relay Chat system of servers. **Internet Relay Chat** or **IRC** has been around since the early days of the Internet. It is made up of servers all over the world that act as hosts for thousands of people to log on and chat.

In IRC, text appears on screen as chatters type and hit return. To use IRC, though, chatters need a program or **client** to connect to their servers. A software program called **mIRC** is among those used for Windows environments and the program **Ircle** is popular on Macintoshes.

IRC offers public, private, and secret rooms. It's like a great big house where people meet to interact. That's a good way to think about it. A public room is open to all—like the first-floor living room. A private room requires an invitation to get in, like a conference room that has a passkey entry system. You need to know the password or name of the room to get in. A secret room may just be a meeting place for two people to talk privately, like that third floor closet where secret discussions are carried out. Sounds like a mystery game, doesn't it?

It's really not mysterious, but just like the real world where a group might meet to chat, a closed meeting might occur or two or more people might meet secretly to discuss private things.

Text-Based Chat

- Basic type of Internet chat
- IRC - Internet Relay Chat
  - mIRC - Windows
  - Ircle - Macintosh
- Text appears on screen as chatters type and hit return
- Public, private, and secret rooms

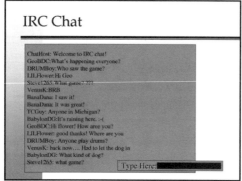

Slide 6: IRC Chat

Here's a sample of what an IRC public room might look like. There might be a host for the room or **channel** in IRC who welcomes people and monitors the activity. Here you see various chatters with their nicknames, talking about different topics or just greeting each other. You'll get a box to type in your own chat and then press return to send the text to the room. Note that I've been saying room a lot already in this talk. When I talk about rooms in the chat environment, I mean the common location that chatters have logged into. It's a cyberroom.

    IRC text scrolls rather quickly if the conversation is in full swing so you have to pay attention.

Slide 7: Web-Based Chat

Web-based chat takes the idea of IRC to a different level. There is no download of an IRC client required. You surf to a Web site that offers chat and a window appears in your Web browser that has many of the same features as IRC.

    Web chats usually run under **Java-enabled features**. Java programs are added to Web pages to make the pages do extra things—like offer a real-time chat or allow you to order merchandise. With Java, you'll get access to the chat, a list of chatters in the room, windows that might contain a private message from another chatter, and informational screens that might provide a profile of a chatter in the room. That profile window may include a picture, some brief information about the person chatting, and links to her own pages on the Web.

    There are many chat sites available on the World Wide Web, at major, multipurpose sites as well as sites devoted to specific topics or just to chat.

Slide 8: Web-Based Chat

Here's a look at our friends we met in IRC. They've moved over to a Web-based chat. Notice we have three windows to look at: the chat window where the text scrolls by; a window that tells us what chat we are in or welcomes us and a left-hand side window that includes a list of who is chatting; and the box to input text and a button to click on to send.

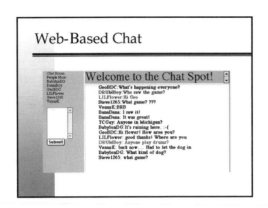

Slide 9: Which Web Sites Have Chat?

Which Web sites have chat features? **Portals** like Yahoo! or Excite have chat features as do many others. Take a look at a site like Talk City for hundreds of chat options or do a search with your favourite search engine to find more.

Slide 10: America Online

We should also mention **America Online,** the US online service that you may have seen ads for. You may have received a disk in the mail to use to get on their system. **AOL** offers some of the easiest-to-use chat rooms around on hundreds of topics every day. You must subscribe to their service, however, because it's not free like most of the Web-based chat sites.

Slide 11: Instant Messaging

A newer form of real-time interaction on the Net is **Instant Messaging.** Instant messaging involves using a client program again to connect you to the Internet. You may have your IM software configured to show when your friends are on—that's called a **Buddy List** on some systems like America Online.

You might hear your friend Doug say that one of his friends in San Francisco sent him an IM while he was

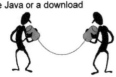

online. That means that they were both logged into the IM system when the friend in California noticed Doug was on and sent him an instant message. They could have a conversation that way over the Internet, IMing back and forth.

It's interesting to note that IM software lets people know when you come online if you are on their buddy list, so you might be giving up some privacy.

You are also able to exchange files such as pictures while using an IM program. We have a sampling of some of these programs coming up that you might want to try out.

IM access might be Java-based in the Web environment or a download of a small program.

Instant Messaging

- Popular Clients/Software
  - ICQ ("I seek you")
  - Yahoo Pager
  - MSN Messenger
  - AOL Instant Messenger

Slide 12: Instant Messaging

Popular clients or software for instant messaging is listed here.

ICQ, or "I seek you," is one of the widely-used IM clients and it allows many features we've mentioned, such as file transfers and user buddy lists. You may see Web sites for persons who list their e-mail address and their **ICQ number**. That's their identifying number on the ICQ system.

Yahoo Pager, MSN Messenger and the prominent **AOL Instant Messenger** round out the choices for this type of chat.

Emerging Methods

- Graphical chat
- Avatars
- Voice chat via Internet
- Video chat

Slide 13: Emerging Methods

There are some emerging methods of chatting that have become more popular in the last few years or are starting to gain popularity. Let's take a look at them.

Slide 14: Avatars

Some Java-enabled Web chats take the graphical interface to new heights using **virtual reality** environments and something called **avatars**. Virtual reality might be a graphical representation of a room that looks just like a real room on your screen. Your graphic chat persona, or avatar, is a representation of you moving in the chat room. An avatar might be a picture of your face or some other graphic that represents you in the chat environment. This gentleman on the slide is Adam and he uses this picture for his avatar in chat rooms that utilize graphics.

Are you curious about avatars? There is a thriving community of people doing work with avatars and virtual environments on the Web. I did a Web search before the class and found many links to follow to find out more.

Slide 15: Video Chats

Video chats have been around awhile but the technology is improving rapidly.

Have you heard of **CU See Me**? It's a program that came from Cornell University in the early '90s. Users with little cameras attached to their computers connect to each other or to servers that allow a group of people to see each other at the same time. It's a form of videoconferencing.

Many sites cater to those who have **Web cams**, the next generation of the little cameras we just mentioned, that allow you to chat with a group or one on one and see faces as well. You may even be able to speak into the camera's microphone or your computer's microphone and have the other person hear you.

Here's our friend Adam again on his own Web cam, ready to talk with whomever might be in the chat area.

This is the obvious next step in chatting on the Net. We went from text to slicker Web interfaces to the use of cameras and microphones for actual face-to-face communication. Of course, it's all dependent on the speed and quality of your Internet connection.

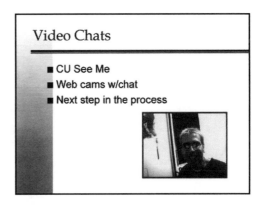

```
┌─────────────────────────────────────┐
│  Types of Chat Rooms                 │
│ ─────────────────────────────────    │
│                                      │
│   ■ General interest                 │
│   ■ Software/hardware help           │
│   ■ Specific topic                   │
│     – health concerns/support        │
│     – popular culture                │
│   ■ Romance and dating               │
│   ■ Sexual interests                 │
│                                      │
└─────────────────────────────────────┘
```

Slide 16: Types of Chat Rooms

Here are some of the types of chat rooms you'll find on Web sites or on AOL.

General interest rooms are meeting places for people to talk about whatever they'd like. Sometimes they are starting points where chatters look for other rooms to visit. Sometimes they are called lobbies.

Software/hardware help rooms cater to people who have specific needs or questions about their computers. What better place than on a PC to find people willing to answer a question or two or point you to a site to find answers.

Specific topics might range from investments to orchid growing. For just about every interest in the world, you'll find a group willing to gather in a chat room and talk. There's a key point as well: chatting is global. You may find yourself chatting with people from all over the world who have the same interests as you.

People with health concerns can find support and help in chat rooms related to their specific issue, from diabetes or cancer to psychological needs. Remember, though, that this type of chat should just be for support and not an actual medical answer to your needs.

In the realm of popular culture, chat rooms thrive on topics like *The X-Files* and musical artists or groups. Many chatters log on right after their favourite show to discuss the episode and trade opinions.

There is an active group of people seeking romance in chat rooms. It is not uncommon for two people to establish a cyberrelationship, complete with online dates and courtship.

Which leads us to the fact that sexual interests are prominent on many chat sites and AOL. Be aware that you can venture into many rooms with a romantic heading that may be rather sexual in nature. Have you heard the term **cybersex**? That means that two people are discussing sexual matters via a private chat.

Any questions?

<Allow audience to respond.>

Slide 17: Auditorium Chats

Many chat sites and AOL feature auditorium chats where notable personalities talk with fans. A regular chat room might hold 30 people. An auditorium chat might accommodate 300. Authors, movie, and television personalities, and sports figures make "personal" appearances this way, fielding moderated questions from the audience.

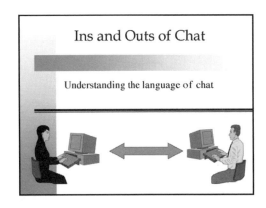

Auditorium Chats

- Notable personalities talk with fans online in large chat environments.

Slide 18: Ins and Outs of Chat

Let's take a look at some of the terms associated with chatting. Sometimes they can be confusing to those who haven't participated or are new to chat. Do you know what a **newbie** is? It's a person new to chat or some other Internet feature. How many chat newbies do we have in the room?

<Allow audience to respond.>

Ins and Outs of Chat

Understanding the language of chat

Slide 19: Chat Terms Defined

Here are some more terms you may see in the chat rooms.

Lag is the time between typing your message and when it appears on screen. "We have a long lag tonight" means the chat server or system may be working slowly causing the conversations to crawl.

A **lurker** is someone who's in the chat but never "speaks," just reads the other chatters' conversations.

Your **Nick** is your chat nickname. If I'm a big fan of *The X-Files*, I might have a chat nickname like MulderRules or ScullyFan. A nickname might pertain to any part of your life, your career, or your interests.

Chat Terms Defined

- Lag - Time between typing your message and when it appears on screen
- Lurker - someone who's in the chat but never "speaks"
- Newbie - Someone new to an online service
- Nick - your chat nickname

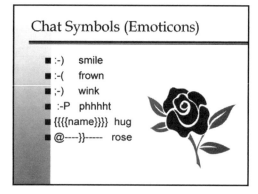

Slide 20: Chat Symbols (Emoticons)

This is one of my favourites. Here are some symbols you might have seen in chat or even in an e-mail. These are also called emoticons and are made by using some of the symbol keys on your computer keyboard. See how the colon, dash, and close parenthesis make a sideways smile?

The face with the capital P means we might be sticking our tongue out at someone playfully.

A chat nickname enclosed in brackets is a hug for that person. You might get a hug when you enter a chat room or return to one after being gone for a while.

Finally, we use the @ (at) symbol and dashes to make a rose. You might send someone a rose in chat or in an e-mail.

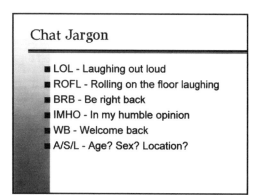

Slide 21: Chat Jargon

Here is some jargon defined as well. Have you seen these in chats or in an e-mail? You may think of reasons to use each of these while chatting. They save time, allow you to respond to a joke, or let people know that you are leaving your PC for a few minutes.

The A/S/L is a question often asked in chat. Someone wants to know how old you are, what gender you are, and where you are. Say only what you want to in chat.

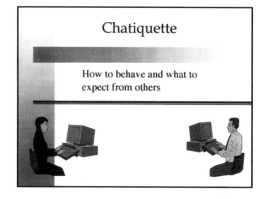

Slide 22: Chatiquette

You may have heard of netiquette, the way to conduct yourself online. Netiquette for chat is called **Chatiquette**. Here are some tips.

Slide 23: Getting Started

When you get into chat for the first time follow these rules.

Lurk for a while until you understand the rules of the room. Some chat rooms have unspoken guidelines, like not asking that A/S/L question, or staying on the room's topic. Participate when you're ready.

Be cautious about personal questions from anyone in private chat or in the room "What's your address?" and "What's your phone number?" are questions you need not answer unless you really and truly want the person to call you. If you are inclined to meet in person someone from chat who lives in your town, meet in public. Do not give out your address unless you know the person.

You may want to trade videotapes or collectibles with others in a group of fans of some celebrity. That may be an okay time to give out your address. Establish some trust first, though.

> **Getting Started**
> - Lurk for a while.
> - Participate when you're ready and understand the rules of the chat room.
> - Be cautious.
>   - "What's your address?"
>   - "What's your phone number?"

Slide 24: Chat is Anonymous

In fact, ask yourself this: With whom are you chatting? Do you really know? It's easy to fake an identity in chat because chat is so anonymous. A 45-year-old man could pose as a 16-year-old girl or vice versa.

If you are female, you may be accosted by men who want to talk. They may even make you uncomfortable. You do not have to engage with anyone you do not want to.

> **Chat is Anonymous**
> - It's easy to fake an identity.
> - Females may be accosted.

Slide 25: In the Chat Environment

In chat, then, you may find that conversations are hard to follow. You may also find that some chat members can be rude or unfriendly. They may even be offensive. You can always ignore them or leave the room for another chat.

Be prepared in certain rooms for frank discussions about sex and other topics. Sometimes people feel as though they can say anything they want in a chat room

> **In the Chat Environment**
> - Expect disjointed conversations.
> - Some people are rude.
> - Some people are offensive.
> - Expect frank discussions.

because they are safe behind their PCs and anonymous chat names.

Slide 26: Tips for Chatting

Here are some tips for chatting that will help make your chat experience pleasant and make the rooms you visit pleasant as well. Some of these we've already touched on. Of course, do not be one of the offensive people in the room. In so many of the environments of the Internet, the Golden Rule applies. Be nice!

Do not **flame** others. Flaming is insulting words directed at another person on the Internet in chat or in an e-mail.

And do not type in all caps because that's the equivalent of shouting in the chat room. People may write back "Why are you shouting?"

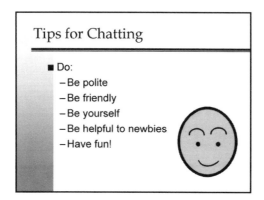

Slide 27: Tips for Chatting

Finally, here are some definite "dos" for chatting. As you can see, they all remind us of the Golden Rule. Be kind. Be nice. Help newbies when you are an experienced chat room user. And be sure to have fun.

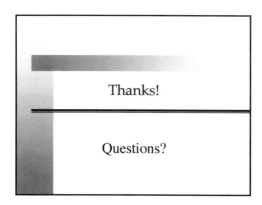

Slide 28: Thanks!

We've reached the end. Thanks. Questions?

Module 10
Surfing Safe!
Children and Their Parents on the World Wide Web

INTRODUCTION

Horror stories of Internet predators appear in the media, scaring some parents away from allowing their children to use the Internet or have access at home. Internet predators are a real danger. Parents can take simple steps, however, to ensure their children are surfing safely and taking advantage of some of the terrific resources the Net has to offer.

Some outstanding Web sites and publications provide safe surfing tips. The Centre for Europe's Children provides a useful Web site regarding the safety of children on the Internet at *www.eurochild.gla.ac.uk/library/SafetyLibrary.htm.*

Frances Walters, Head of Children's Services at SJCPL, has presented a class called *Internet for Kids and Parents* for a number of years. Devoted to Web basics, surfing, searching, and evaluation of Web sites, the class also contains a section on safe use for children. She urges parents to be aware and involved in what their children are doing with the Web. Her main point: The Internet can be fun and educational and doesn't have to be scary. "Parents," she says in the class, "there is, at this time, no foolproof way to protect your children from sites that may be objectionable. You might want to discuss with your children what is and is not acceptable for them, as well as what to do if they come across 'bad' sites."

The audience for this module consists of parents and other concerned adults.

WORKSHOP ATTENDEES WILL GAIN:

1. An understanding of the basics of the Internet and the World Wide Web as an educational tool and source of entertainment for young people.
2. An examination of safe surfing guidelines for children and parents.
3. An opportunity to explore the Web for more information with suggested URLs.
4. An opportunity to discuss these issues with other parents and librarians.

TIPS FOR PRESENTING THIS MODULE

- Larry Magid offers a free download of the entire *Child Safety on the Information Highway* booklet at *www.safekids.com/presentation.htm* as a PowerPoint presentation. His rules are simple: You can add but don't change any slides and let him know how it goes. You might present this module (with the three slides devoted to Magid's work removed) and then present his as well.
- Alternatively, you may wish to make reference to the conference slides on 'Child safety on the Internet—Developing Policy and Practice' at *www/eurochild.gla.ac.uk/News_Events/Conferences/InternetSafety Conf.htm*
- I e-mailed Larry Magid asking how librarians can get copies of his work to distribute. He wrote back: "The printed version is available from the National Center for Missing and Exploited Children. For details, call 800–THE LOST. Of course, people can always print it out from SafeKids.Com."
- A children's librarian can take children for their own Internet basics session or storytime while parents are in this class.
- Provide books and magazines on Internet topics for children and parents that can be checked out after class.
- This is one of the shorter modules in the *Toolkit*. It is designed to allow time after the presentation for a facilitated discussion led by the presenter or another expert, librarian, or teacher. Parents may have questions or concerns they would like to voice.

MODULE 10—SURFING SAFE! CHILDREN AND THEIR PARENTS ON THE WORLD WIDE WEB—SCRIPT

Slide 1: Introduction

<Introduce yourself, your assisting expert, and helper if you have one. Tell the group that you will be using a presentation program called PowerPoint to present the programme.>

Surfing Safe! Children and Their Parents on the World Wide Web

<Your Name Here>
<Your Library Name Here>

Slide 2: Our Checklist

Here's our checklist for this class. We will cover the Internet as community and as educational tool for children. Then we'll look at some important safe-surfing tips for children as well as tips for parents.

Our Checklist

- The Internet
  - As community
  - As educational tool
- Surfing tips for children
- Tips for parents

Slide 3: The Internet as Community

If you have surfed the Web or taken other classes with us, you may have learned how similar the Internet and World Wide Web are to a global community wired together through networks of computers.

That community is made up of diverse people from all over the world. You may have discovered Web sites devoted to your favourite topic or chat rooms where your hobby is actively discussed. You may have discovered Web pages that provide information on your favourite artist or author or how to grow the perfect rose.

There is something for almost everyone on the Internet, including our children.

The Internet as Community

- Global neighbourhood
- Connected cities and towns
- Something for almost everyone

The Internet for Children

- Children's Web sites
- Chat rooms for children
- Fun and games
- Academic pursuits

Slide 4: The Internet for Children

We'll find Web sites catering to children on almost any topic. There are chat sites just for children. There are a lot of game sites and sites devoted to pure fun. We'll also find sites that have a more academic focus for children.

The Internet as Educational Tool

- Online learning
- Current events
- Homework help
- Virtual Library

Slide 5: The Internet as Educational Tool

That's our second point for the class: The Internet offers many interesting and educational sites for children to assist them with school and learning. Using the Web offers children an engaging way to learn. Sometimes they're learning and having fun at the same time.

<If you have such a programme at your library, mention a recent children's Internet activity you've done. Add a slide or two of digital pictures of the children learning in your library with the Web, if you have them. >

Online Learning

- Many Web sites for children offer games, learning modules, and online quizzes.

Slide 6: Online Learning

Some Web sites offer games, learning modules, and online quizzes. For example, online modules concerning the planets teach the topic and then quiz the child to test what she has learned about Jupiter or Mars. These sites might have been developed by educators for their classes and posted on the Web for all to use.

Current Events

- Web sites offer the news
  - www.bbc.co.uk
  - www.cnn.com
  - www.kidsclick.org

Slide 7: Current Events

The Web features sites that cover current events in great detail from many different news organizations. The BBC puts much of the day's issue up for perusal on the Web. CNN offers breaking news as it happens. Children can follow news stories of interest to them or stories assigned by their teachers and watch the details change as breaking stories occur.

The site *www.kidsclick.org* offers links to current events and many more topics.

Slide 8: Homework Help

The Web offers a huge amount of homework help for children. Sites like Britannica and the CIA World Factbook provide accurate and useful information for reports on any number of topics from inventors to historical figures or reports on various countries of the world.

Slide 9: Virtual Library

In fact, the Web could be called a huge virtual library, not only for young people but all of us. Just like our library has an adult book area and a children's area, so does the Web. As I mentioned before, sites on almost any topic are available through the World Wide Web. Your child might need to study bats and find plans for a bat house for a class report. A simple search at a site like Google, which we'll talk about a bit later, yields a handful of useful places to look for design plans.

Slide 10: Portals and Lists Point the Way

How do we get our kids started on the Web? An excellent starting point is to use a Web portal or a subject list. A Web portal offers an entry to different sites on the Web. Portals are usually like a "one-stop shopping" spot for everything you might want to access. Free e-mail, Web chat, auctions, news, weather, personals, horoscopes, stock info, and more are found on portals.

Portals and Lists Point the Way

Yahooligans! - www.yahooligans.com
· Open Directory - www.dmoz.org
· Government Sites - www.explore.parliament.uk
· Library sites
  – <Your Library>
  – St. Joseph County Public Library

Slide 11: Yahooligans! Screenshot

Some portals like Yahoo! have created their own children's version. Yahoo!'s is called Yahooligans! This version of Yahoo! is created especially for young people, with graphics that are sometimes silly and fun. Note the various links to games, school information, and Harry Potter.

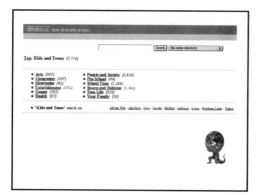

Slide 12: Open Directory Project Screenshot

Subject lists, which are well-organized guides to the Web, are also valuable starting points. The Open Directory Project at *www.dmoz.org* offers streamlined pages of links for children and teens.

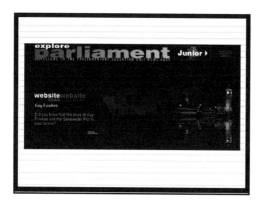

Slide 13: Explore Parliament

The Parliamentary Education Unit has an "Explore Parliament" site at *www.explore.parliament.uk*, with games, information, search facilities, news and a teachers' guide.

Slide 14: Homework Zone

<Highlight your library here by changing the screenshots to your own pages and discussing your own offerings. >

Public libraries like our library and the St. Joseph County Public Library in Indiana create sites like "Homework Help" and "Fun and Games" to guide kids to fun and useful sites.

Slide 15: Search Engines Locate Info

Search Engines Locate Info

- Ask Jeeves for Kids - www.ajkids.com
- AltaVista - www.altavista.com
- Google - www.google.com

For finding stuff on the Internet, show children sites like Google, a search engine that gets great results more often than not. The popular Ask Jeeves search engine offers a version at *www.ajkids.com* that pulls back results for young people.

Slide 16: Surfing Tips for Children

There's a lot out there on the Web for children. But how do we make sure our children are surfing safely? The rest of our programme tonight will focus on tips first for the little people in our lives and then for us as parents, grandparents, or concerned adults.

Slide 17: Larry Magid's SafeKids.Com

Los Angeles Times columnist Larry Magid has a site called SafeKids.Com that presents a guide for children and parents, including "My Tips for Online Safety." Many libraries and schools have utilized Larry Magid's work. This evening we have copies of his pamphlet for you to take home, but let's discuss some of the tips now.
<You may also wish to refer to 'Safe surfing for kids' at http://kotn.ntu.ac.uk/safety.htm>

Slide 18: Screenshot of SafeKids.Com

<Update this text/slide as needed as the site changes.>

And here is his site. Take a look at it after class or next time you are on the Internet for more valuable information on this topic. You can even subscribe to his free "Safe Kids" newsletter.

Slide 19: Safety Tips Include

Here's the first tip.
   "I will not give out personal information without my parents' permission."
   That information might be the child's address, telephone number, his parents' work address or telephone number, or the name and location of his school. In the course of chatting in a chat room, a child may innocently tell someone where he lives or what school he

goes to. That information is best kept private, not only from sexual predators that could be in the room but from other unscrupulous Internet users.

Slide 20: Safety Tips Include:

Here's another tip.

"I will tell my parents right away if I come across any information that makes me feel uncomfortable."

Let your children know it's okay to tell you that they stumbled into something that was scary or of an adult nature while surfing. When you are searching, it is easy to sometimes be accidentally led into an adult site. It happens to adults too—sometimes while we're at work and usually when someone happens to be passing by!

Slide 21: Tips for Parents

Now let's look at some tips for parents who are struggling with the idea of their children going online.

Slide 22: Parents

Parents: The Internet is NOT populated solely with paedophiles and predators. The media will play up stories involving children that have been lured into meeting an adult or into something unpleasant. *Time* magazine had a cover story a few years ago that featured cover art of a frightened child and a menacing computer. It is not that bad. The Internet is wonderful and diverse and full of interesting topics to pursue, as we mentioned at the start of the programme.

But there is some danger. Sites like SafeKids.Com wouldn't exist if the danger wasn't there.

Your awareness is the key, and you're taking a good first step by coming to this class. Common sense should prevail when dealing with children and the Internet.

And a little guidance goes a long way. There are many organizations and Web sites available to do just that.

Slide 23: BECTa Internet Safety Guides for Children

BECTa, the British Education Communications and Technology agency, provides useful information on Internet Safety Guidelines for children, as a result of their Internet Safety Seminar held in March 2001. Notes from presentations are available for download from their site at *www.becta.org.uk/technology/safetyseminar/index.html*.

A good site for children to start exploring the Internet is the Yahoo! site 'Yahooligans' at *www.yahooligans.com*.

You might also talk to your children about Web sites and what makes a good one.

Slide 24: Evaluation Tips for Children

A tip from the American Library Association (ALA) is "Not everything on the Web is true. Some information could be false or misleading." Sometimes both children and adults think that if it's on the Web it must be true or factual, but that's not always the case.

It might be worth discussing the whole question of authority with older children. For example, if they are doing a report on space travel and planets it might be better to go to NASA instead of a site whose author is unknown.

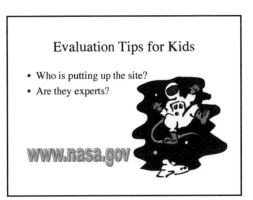

Evaluation Tips for Kids

- Some sites are just advertisements.
- Others offer good information or resources.

Tips for Parents

- A portion of the World Wide Web is violent, obscene, or scary.
- But that's just a small portion!

Tips for Parents

- It's a good idea to place computers in the kitchen, family room, or living room so that you can see your child using it.

Slide 25: Evaluation Tips for Kids

Discuss with your child that some Web sites are just advertisements for products or shows, while others offer good information and resources. And let her know that both are good, but there is a difference.

The happy hippo cartoon character may be your child's favourite but may just be selling his merchandise online and not offering what other sites do, such as educational games or learning with similar characters. A site such as Blue Peter at *www.bbc.co.uk/cbbc/bluepeter/* may provide more informative and educational material than a site dedicated to a child's favourite cartoon character.

Slide 26: Tips for Parents

Let's take a look at another tip. This one is for parents and it reinforces what we've been discussing about the usefulness of the Web.

"A portion of the World Wide Web is violent, obscene, or scary. But that's just a small portion!"

Just like in the real world, there are parts of the online community not intended for young people. There are some sites that appeal to only a few people and that might scare others. Know that these sites are out there, but remember the first part of our class: The Internet is vast and filled with useful and fun places to visit.

Slide 27: Tips for Parents

Here's another tip to think about. Where is your computer at home? Is it tucked away in a seldom-used room or in your child's bedroom?

A PC in your home's common area not only ensures that you'll know what your kids are up to online, but it will also promote interaction with your kids. They may feel more comfortable asking questions or for help if you are readily available.

Slide 28: Other Tips for Parents

One more tip.

"If you have a home PC, software filters are available to block Web sites you may not want your child to visit."

Some parents, schools, and libraries use filtering software to insure safe access to Web sites without the danger of unpleasant or adult content getting through.

> **Other Tips for Parents**
>
> • If you have a home PC, software filters are available to block Web sites you may not want your child to visit.

Slide 29: Filters

What are filters exactly? For home use, there is software that blocks certain Web sites based on predefined cues or words. For example, a filter might block all sites that contain references to four-letter words we won't mention here.

Filters are not perfect. They sometimes block important stuff, like information on safe sex. A teen in your life may want to know about safe sex, STDs, or being gay and being afraid to talk to anyone about it. There's a lot of information and support on the Web, but a filter may block it.

As parents, you can control what is blocked by tweaking the software's settings. For example, some filters can be set to allow certain topics through but not others. Some of these topics include sex, gambling, drugs, hate sites, and school cheating sites. As parents, you can decide what's acceptable on your home PC.

The ALA stance on filters is that they can be used but they are "no substitute for parental guidance."

> **Filters**
>
> • Software filters block certain Web sites.
> • They are not perfect.
> • Parents can control what is blocked.
> • ALA: "No substitute for parental guidance."

Slide 30: A Few More Tips

We'll find a lot of other sites that offer advice and tips to parents and children about the Net if we search or follow any of the URLs discussed tonight. Here are a few more tips.

> **A Few More Tips**
>
>

Discuss Netiquette

- Practice the Golden Rule
- Rudeness breeds rudeness
- DON'T TYPE IN ALL CAPS

Slide 31: Discuss Netiquette

Teach your child about netiquette. That's etiquette for the Internet. Tell her it's like playing with friends or going on a shopping trip: be friendly, courteous, and kind.

In chat or in e-mail, tell her not to use all caps. Does anyone know what that means?

<Allow audience to respond.>

Right—that's the Net equivalent of shouting.

E-mail Tip

- For safety's sake, your child should use a nickname rather than his real name when sending e-mail.

Slide 32: E-mail Tip

A general e-mail tip:

"For safety's sake, your child should use a nickname rather than his real name when sending e-mail."

That protects the child from having someone he doesn't know find out too much about him. Even his first name could be an "in" for a predator on the Web. Make choosing an online name a game with your child. Does he like a certain character or hobby? Build the name from that interest.

Chat Tips

- All of the guidelines apply.
- Chatting should be fun - not scary.
- Predators are not in every chat room!

Slide 33: Chat Tips

Here are a few tips for chat rooms. All of the guidelines we've discussed in this class apply. Don't give out too much info. Instruct your child to leave the room if something makes her uncomfortable and to tell you about it.

Chatting should be fun for kids, not scary in any way. Sometimes it seems like we always hear about the bad things that happen to children in chat rooms. Predators are not in every chat room, but it's wise to be cautious. Check out SafeKids.Com info on safe chatting and the perils of chat rooms.

<See the chat module in the Toolkit *for more information.>*

Slide 34: "Sesame Street" Tips

The people at "Sesame Street" offer some great tips for parents as well. They emphasize that "parents must always know 'where' their children are, on- and offline."

That's common sense. We probably wouldn't want our ten-year-old out and about late at night in a strange city. The same can be said for roaming around the Web.

Parents should regularly discuss the Internet with their kids. Make it fun. Ask them what their favourite sites are and go there with them. Include in that discussion some of our points from this class and the booklet. Stay involved and have fun with your children as they grow up as savvy Net users.

"Sesame Street" Tips

- Parents must always know "where" their children are, on- and offline.
- Parents should regularly discuss the Internet with their kids.

www.sesameworkshop.org/parents

Slide 35: Useful Links

Once again, here are some useful links we've touched on. And with that we've reached the end of our presentation. Questions?

Useful Links

- www.safekids.com
- www.safeteens.com
- www.safesurfin.com

Slide 36: Thanks!

<Close with questions, start the discussion, or introduce your expert facilitator with a set time frame: "Let's discuss any issues you have on this topic for the next 20 minutes and then we'll get you back together with your children....">

Thanks!

Questions?

Module 11
Selling and Saving: Exploring WWW Auctions

INTRODUCTION

Auctions on the World Wide Web exploded on the cyberlandscape in 1997 and 1998. eBay™, still number one according to the Top 100 Auction Sites Web site, opened a whole new arena for the Web: selling your stuff for fun and profit. Internet savvy auctioneers discovered that their trash was someone else's treasure. The Garfield teapot from 1981 that seemed to be a white elephant suddenly became a valuable collectible, selling for $84 on eBay™. The knick-knacks cluttering shelves and packed away in basements became sought-after items.

I watched eBay™ with interest in 1998 and actually sold my first item in May of that year (the teapot mentioned above). Since then, we have introduced eBay™ in our shopping classes at St. Joseph County Public Library (SJCPL). Recently, I encountered a colleague on break at a public Internet terminal, focused intently on the screen. "Don't bother me," Frank said. "I'm eBaying."

"To eBay™" will probably be added to the dictionary before long. The popularity of that site and other auction sites like Yahoo! and Amazon continues. Books are available on the topic. eBay™ publishes a glossy magazine for users.

Your library users are probably very curious about participating in auctions. This module guides them through the experience.

<You may prefer to refer to the UK version of eBay at www.ebay.co.uk *throughout this presentation.>*

WORKSHOP ATTENDEES WILL GAIN:

1. An understanding of how online auction sites work.
2. An overview of the steps taken to participate at sites like eBay™ and Yahoo!
3. Some tips to get the most out of selling or buying at cyberauctions.

TIPS FOR PRESENTING THIS MODULE

- Take the class online and demonstrate eBay™ or another site. I have used the following examples to show what's available.
- Choose a popular clothes designer—Calvin Klein, Ralph Lauren, Kenneth Cole—and demonstrate how clothing and accessories are sold.
- Ask your audience for suggestions that you can search for if you are doing a live session.
- Alternatively, choose a couple of items that are of interest to your audience.

MODULE 11—SELLING AND SAVING: EXPLORING WWW AUCTIONS

Slide 1: Introduction

<Introduce yourself and your helper if you have one. Tell the group that you will be using a presentation program called PowerPoint to present the programme.>

> **Selling and Saving:**
> **Exploring WWW Auctions**
>
> <Your Name Here>
> <Your Library Name Here>

Slide 2: Trash or Treasure?

In this class, we're going to discuss the world of online auction. Online auctions sites are like a huge, global car-boot sale where practically anything is up for bids!

> **Trash or Treasure?**
>
> Online auctions sites are like a global car-boot sale where anything is up for bids!

Slide 3: Online Auctions

Here's our plan for the class. Before we start, has anyone sold anything on an online auction? Or maybe bought something?

<Allow audience to respond.>

> **Online Auctions**
>
> • What's an online auction?
> • What's it like to participate?
> • Tips for safe selling
> • Tips for safe bidding

What's an online auction?

- Web sites designed to sell items via bids
- Items listed with photos and information
- Sellers and buyers dealing directly

Slide 4: What's an online auction?

An online auction takes place on a Web site designed to sell items by taking bids. Just as an auctioneer listens and watches a crowd at a live auction, an auction site monitors the amount of a bid and keeps track of who's winning.

Items are listed with photos and information that visitors to the sites can search and browse. Search features at eBay™ or Yahoo! auctions allow surfers to locate exactly what they want to bid on.

Sellers and buyers deal directly with each other. There is no middleman at online auctions, other than the small percentage that some sites take to list and sell an item. It makes virtually the whole world one big flea market.

What's an online auction?

- Auction has beginning and ending times
- Multiple items are available at the same time
- Bidders can find practically anything

Slide 5: What's an online auction?

Auctions online have predetermined beginning and ending times. That means that the auction might begin at 1 p.m. on Saturday and run for seven days until 1 p.m. the next Saturday.

Unlike the live auction you might attend, multiple items are available at the same time on the auction sites. There might be over five million items for sale at any given time on a site like eBay™. Bidders can find practically anything.

Practically Anything?

- Collectibles
- Antiques
- Memorabilia
- Clothing
- Electronics
- Music, movies, and games

Slide 6: Practically Anything?

Practically anything? Yes, just about any type of item can be found for sale on auction sites. Take a look at this list. We might search and find the perfect addition to our collection of salt and pepper shakers, an antique set of linens, a poster of a 1977 Fleetwood Mac concert, a brand-new Calvin Klein dress, a digital camera, or our favourite movie on DVD.

Slide 7: Popular Auction Sites

Here are some of the most popular auction sites. You may recognize some of these names.

Specialized sites offer auctions for particular kinds of items, such as china or movie collectibles. The last URL points you to the top 100 auction sites on the Web.

> **Popular Auction Sites**
>
> - eBay™   www.ebay.com
> - Yahoo! auctions.yahoo.com
> - Amazon   www.auctions.amazon.com
> - Bidder's Edge www.biddersedge.com
> - Specialized sites
> - Top 100   www.100topauctionsites.com

Slide 8: eBay™ Screenshot

That site, the Top 100 list, ranks eBay™ as the number one auction site on the Web. According to the site history, eBay™ was founded in September 1995 and has 27.9 million registered users. It is one of the most popular shopping sites on the Internet. Here's a shot of the main page. Note that there are categories to choose from, featured items, a search box, and lots of help for buyers and sellers. This is a well-planned, friendly site to use.

Slide 9: How Auction Sites Work

Let's go a little deeper and look at how an auction site works. Here is a step-by-step breakdown of what happens when an auction takes place. Sellers and buyers must establish an account with whatever auction site they are going to use. Sellers then list items that buyers browse and bid on. When the auction ends, the highest bid wins.

Then—

> **How Auction Sites Work**
>
> - Sellers and buyers establish an account
> - Sellers list items (fees?)
> - Buyers make bids
> - Highest bid wins when auction closes

Slide 10: How Auction Sites Work

The site automatically notifies the buyer and seller that the auction has ended. The seller e-mails the buyer a bill for the total amount for the item and any shipping charges. The buyer pays the seller for the item. The seller ships the item to the buyer. Finally, the seller and buyer post feedback about each other.

> **How Auction Sites Work**
>
> - Site notifies participants
> - Seller e-mails buyer
> - Buyer pays seller for item plus shipping
> - Seller ships the item to buyer
> - Seller and buyer post feedback

How Auction Sites Make Money

- Sites like eBay™ charge a listing fee
- When auction closes they take a small percentage
- Fees are charged to credit cards

Slide 11: How Auction Sites Make Money

You might be wondering how the auction sites make money. A site like eBay™, for example, charges a small fee to list an item. That's called an insertion fee. eBay™'s site describes an insertion fee as "usually between £0.15p and £1.25p, depending on the opening bid."

Then there is a final sale price fee at the end of the auction. eBay™ states that the fee generally ranges from 1.25 percent to 5 percent of the final sale price.

The site will charge your credit card once a month for any final auction percentages you owe them. It's a reasonably smooth system.
(Source: *http://pages.ebay.co.uk/help/index.html*)

Let's look at some of the steps for participating in online auctions more closely.

Establishing an Account

- Sites like eBay™ may require:
  - Name
  - Address
  - E-mail address
  - Phone
  - Credit card information
  - Username

Slide 12: Establishing an Account

When you establish an account with one of the sites we've mentioned, you are asked to provide some personal information. This is important because it is in fact a marketplace where honesty counts. Sites like eBay™ may require your full name, your address, your e-mail address, your phone number, and your credit card information.

You will also establish a username for the site. It might be your e-mail address or a nickname you use online.

Is it a little scary to give out that much information? Don't worry. Sites like eBay™ protect their users' privacy as much as possible, and credit card numbers are totally secure. A user can request the contact info for a seller, but he must provide his own contact info as well. For example, if I request from eBay™ the phone number of a seller, that seller is sent an e-mail stating that I had requested it and eBay™ provided it.

Slide 13: Listing an Item

When listing an item for bidding, you make many decisions about that item. All of these things listed can be set by you, according to the site guidelines.

For example—

> **Listing an Item**
>
> • You decide
>   – Type of auction
>   – Length of auction
>   – Item category
>   – Item description
>   – Item photo
>   – Minimum price
>   – Opening bid

Slide 14: Types of Auctions

Types of auctions include reserve price, Dutch, private, and restricted.

A **reserve price auction** is one where you set a minimum price that you will sell for. For example, I might not want to sell my portable player for anything less than £50, so I set a reserve of £50 for it. You can also choose to price your item in £ or $. If selling in the UK, it is sensible to price in £, but if you wish to attract overseas buyers it may be more sensible to price in $.

A **Dutch auction** is one that has many of the same item for sale. Buyers can bid on a certain amount of that item. For example, I have ten packages of computer disks I got at a computer show for a great price. I put them up for Dutch auction and invite buyers to bid on how many packages they want and how much they want to pay for each package.

A **private auction** hides the usernames of the bidders from other people looking at the auction. That's to protect the privacy of certain auctions and at the seller's discretion.

> **Types of Auctions**
>
> • Reserve price
> • Dutch
> • Private

Slide 15: Length of Auction

As a seller, you also set the length of the auction. The standard for eBay™ is seven days, but some auction can be set for three or ten days or defined solely by the seller.

If you talk with people who sell a lot on the auction sites about auction duration, many say the seven-day length is good because it allows enough time for people visiting the site to find their items. Three days some-

> **Length of Auction**
>
> • 7 days (standard for eBay™)
> • 3 days
> • 10 days

times is too short, unless it's a hot item like the Sony PlayStation 2 was in the winter of 2000/2001.

Slide 16: Item Details

Sellers also list the item details, including important facts like size, condition, if it works, if it doesn't, and anything else they can think of.

I might list a first edition of Stephen King's *The Shining*. It would be in my best interest to describe the book fully: Are all the pages there, is it damaged, what kind of shape is it in, and so forth.

Item Details

- Size
- Condition
- Anything and everything about the item

Slide 17: Bidding on an Item

Here's how a buyer makes her bid on an item. After locating the perfect piece of china to complete my set by searching the site, I enter my account information and my bid. The system immediately reports back if the bid is the highest so far. If someone has outbid me, I can re-enter a higher amount.

Bidding on an Item

- Buyer locates item
- Inputs account information
- Enters bid
- System reports if bid is highest so far
- Bidder can enter new bid later if outbid

Slide 18: Proxy Bidding

Proxy bidding means a buyer can submit a maximum bid amount and the auction site's computer will act as a proxy for her. In her absence, the system bids for them, trying to keep the auction price as low as possible. This way a buyer doesn't have to be watching that particular auction every minute.

Proxy Bidding

- The auction system watches the bidding for you, increasing your bid in increments until it reaches your maximum amount.

Slide 19: When the Auction Closes

When the auction closes, the highest bidder wins if the reserve price is met. If no one has bid or if the reserve price is not met, the seller may relist the item. Sometimes it might take a couple of weeks to sell an item depending on how many people see the item's listing.

> **When the Auction Closes**
>
> - Highest bidder wins if reserve is met
> - Seller may relist item if no bids are received

Slide 20: Direct Contact

After the buyer and seller are notified by the auction site's computer that the auction has ended, the seller e-mails the buyer with the final amount and asks for the buyer's shipping information.

The buyer and seller have direct contact via e-mail, then, for the rest of the transaction, possibly including the seller e-mailing when the item is shipped and the buyer reciprocating by e-mailing the seller that the item was received.

> **Direct Contact**
>
> - Buyer and seller are alerted to auction results via e-mail by auction system
> - Buyer and seller communicate directly by e-mail

Slide 21: Direct Contact

How does the buyer pay for the item?

Some people send cash, but that's not wise to do for larger amounts.

I might send a cheque to the seller. I may have to wait, though, for the cheque to clear before the seller will ship my item. Some auctions are sold in $ prices. Your seller may require a $ cheque, or extra money to cover bank charges for changing a sterling cheque to dollars. If I send a money order, the seller can ship immediately.

We still have to wait for the mail, though, unless we use one of the online payment services like PayPal, Bidpay, or Billpoint.

> **Direct Contact**
>
> - Seller pays for item
>   - Cash
>   - Cheque
>   - Money order
>   - Online payment
> - Buyer receives payment and ships

Online Payment Services

- Bid Pay www.bidpay.com
- BillPoint www.billpoint.com
- PayPal www.paypal.com

Slide 22: Online Payment Services

An online payment service acts as a funds transfer system to pay for auctions. If I have an account with one of them and I win that auction for the china we mentioned before, I can log on to the service and have £15 sent electronically to the seller.

We each need to have an account—the buyer and the seller. The system, which is secure, keeps our bank account information and electronically transfers funds just like some payroll companies do with direct deposit.

The system e-mails both parties that a payment has been made. Using this kind of service can shorten the time a buyer has to wait for the item.

Feedback

- Auction is completed successfully
- Buyer and seller post feedback or ratings
- Bad auction = negative feedback

Slide 23: Feedback

Posting **feedback** after an auction lets others know how well a buyer or seller conducts business. After an auction is completed successfully, the buyer and seller post ratings on each other—positive, negative, or neutral, for example, on eBay™.

If an auction goes badly, either party may post negative feedback. That shows up on the user profile as a negative. There might also be a short comment explaining why the negative was given: didn't ship, item was not as described, and so on. Some buyers and sellers may not want to deal with a person who has negative feedback. A system like eBay™ keeps track of feedback in numbers of positives, negatives, or neutrals. Some users might have feedback ratings in the hundreds or thousands depending on how many auctions they've done.

Slide 24: When Auctions Go Wrong

Here are some reasons why auctions might not work out successfully.

The seller might send multiple e-mails to the buyer but never get a reply, so he relists the item.

Cheques for payment might bounce.

On the buyer's side, he might receive a faulty or misrepresented item. The cool digital watch listed and pictured on an auction site might be much different when you see it in person.

Sadly, some buyers never receive the item at all. All they can do is post negative feedback and report the seller to the auction site's authorities.

Don't let me scare you, though; hundreds of auctions close successfully every day.

> **When Auctions Go Wrong**
>
> - Seller never hears from buyer, relists
> - Cheques bounce
> - Buyer receives faulty or misrepresented item
> - Buyer never receives item at all
>
>

Slide 25: Tips for Sellers

How are we doing? Questions? Are you intrigued by this idea of online buying and selling?

<Allow audience to respond.>

Here are some tips for those of you wanting to sell your stuff on auction sites.

> **Tips for Sellers**

Slide 26: Do You Have Stuff to Sell?

First, determine if you have stuff to sell. Take a look around the house. Clean out the cellar or the loft, take a look in your cupboards. You never know what you might find that might sell on an online auction site. Examine your family heirlooms. Do you really need to keep Great Aunt Matilda's complete set of glassware from the Fifties?

How will you know what will sell? Take a look at the auction sites to get a good idea of what's selling. Pay attention at car-boot sales for things that might sell well at auction. Look at magazines that have articles about successful online auctioneers. Talk to your friends. What have they sold?

> **Do You Have Stuff to Sell?**
>
> - Clean out the cellar, loft, storage room
> - Look in your cupboards
> - Examine those family heirlooms
> - Keep an eye out at car-boot sales
>
>

Research Your Item First

- Check what the item has already sold for
- Check price guides and other books
- Use online forums/lists
- Have valuable items appraised

Slide 27: Research Your Item First

Then research your item or items. Check what the item has already sold for by searching completed items. You can do that on eBay™ and Yahoo! Searching completed auctions gives you a good idea of what your similar item might be worth.

Check price guides and other books for information as well, especially if the item is a collectible or antique. You can visit the library to browse the price guides.

Use online forums or mailing lists too. Post to a forum on Beanies that you have a special limited-edition bear and ask the group what is a good reserve price. Watch out, though, don't take just one person's word; she may want your bear for herself.

Don't hesitate to have valuable items appraised by a professional if you think the item is actually worth a lot. You can still auction it, but you want to be sure to set a fair reserve.

Write a Detailed Description

- Tell potential buyers *EVERYTHING*
  - Condition - wear and tear
  - Dimensions/Sizes
  - Shipping charges
  - Will you ship internationally?

Slide 28: Write a Detailed Description

Here's another tip: Write a detailed description and tell your potential buyers everything you can about the item, like that Stephen King first edition I mentioned before. What is the condition of the item? How much wear and tear is there? Or is it brand new, never used, or never worn if it's an article of clothing.

Be specific about the size of the item. If it's a shirt, is it an L or an XL; take some measurements if need be. If it's a picture frame, what size photo will it hold?

List in your description what the shipping charges are for the item and decide if you want to ship internationally. That involves special packaging, possibly insurance, and filling out forms at the post office. The expense or risk of shipping overseas may not be worth it.

Slide 29: Include a Photograph

Include a photograph with the listing. Photos really help to sell an item. Follow the site's standards for images if they have them. Use clear, detailed images of your items, like these three shirts that were recently sold as a lot.

Be creative too. Get a friend to model that Bruce Oldfield dress you bought at the charity shop or display objects like teapots or glassware with a nice background.

How do you get pictures? Use your digital camera or borrow a friend's camera or shoot a roll of pictures and have them put on a disk. Many photo stores will do that now.

Follow the directions on whatever site you are using to upload the pictures.

Include a Photograph

- Follow site standards
- Capture a clear, detailed image
- Be creative

Slide 30: Photos of Items

Here are some digital photos of clothing offered on eBay™ recently, courtesy of an auction aficionado in Louisville, Kentucky. She found a dressmaker's dummy at a second-hand shop to use instead of a live model.

The boots are displayed on a flat surface with a contrasting background so interested bidders can see the shape and cut easily.

Slide 31: Use the Site's Features

Another tip for sellers is to use the site as much as possible and take advantage of its features like feedback, profiles, and news. You can also set up an "About Me" page at some sites, where you list your username, location, and what you like to buy and sell. This adds to the experience of participating in the online auction community.

Use the Site's Features

- Check feedback for your buyers
- Read current site news
- Set up "About Me" pages

The Golden Rule

- Be courteous and honest
- Do unto others. . .

Slide 32: The Golden Rule

The final tip for sellers is to follow the Golden Rule. Be courteous and honest in your dealings. Try to earn positive feedback from every transaction. If you hit a snag, work to make it right in your buyer's interest and yours. Treat people online the way you want them to treat you.

Tips for Buyers

Slide 33: Tips for Buyers

On the other side of the coin is the buyer. Here are some tips for those of you interested in bidding and hopefully purchasing from an auction site.

Explore Auctions First

- Learn how things work before diving in
- Visit various sites
- Talk to friends and relatives who've had auction experience

Slide 34: Explore Auctions First

Explore online auctions first. Learn the lay of the land and how things work before diving in and bidding. You might watch a couple of auctions that are about to close to see that some auctions have a flurry of bids in the final minutes.

Visit various auction sites to see the similarities and differences of each one. Check out the top sites we've mentioned like eBay™, Amazon, and Yahoo! Search for your favourite thing at each site—Beanies or CDs or whatever—and look at the listings. Compare prices.

Talk to friends and relatives who've had auction experience and ask them to share what they've learned.

Slide 35: Search Smart

Really, we're reviewing some of our sellers' tips because they apply to buyers too. Make sure you use search features and categories for browsing items you might want to bid on. Follow the site's directions to search.

Compare item prices when you search. The same item might sell for £10 or £23 depending on how it was listed. Research the item value online and offline at the library or with friends or professionals as well.

> Search Smart
>
> - Use categories for browsing
> - Use search boxes to locate specific items
> - Compare item prices with searches
> - Research item value online and off

Slide 36: Watch the Details

As a buyer, pay close attention to the details like a seller's feedback rating. If that seller has a few negatives, I probably wouldn't bid. If he has a huge number of positives, I'd be more inclined to bid.

Use online forums like the ones on eBay™ to discuss items and even request items in the "wanted" section. You never know if someone may have something she might put up if you ask for it.

Be sure to factor shipping and handling into your final cost as you ponder bidding on an item. That CD may be only £10 but the seller wants £5 to ship. I could go to my favourite music store and get it for £13, so I'm not saving in that auction.

Decide if you want to purchase from international sellers because shipping from out of the country can be expensive and the mail might not make it all the way from wherever it's coming from. One friend of mine bought a CD from a fellow in Australia and it took weeks to arrive.

> Watch the Details
>
> - Look at feedback
> - Use online forums/lists
> - Factor shipping and handling into your cost
> - Decide if you want to purchase from international sellers

Set a Maximum Bid

- Decide what is the most you will pay
- Enter bid and let proxy bidding work for you

Slide 37: Set a Maximum Bid

You are ready to bid. Decide the most you will pay for an item and enter the bid. Remember proxy bidding? Let it work for you. If you get outbid, you'll get an e-mail from the auction computer and you can go back and bid again—if you want to spend more money.

The Golden Rule

- Be courteous and honest
- Do unto others. . .

Slide 38: The Golden Rule

We've seen this before. Buyers, the same applies to you. Be courteous in your dealings with sellers. Establish good feedback and build on it.

Finally

- Have fun! There will always be more items.

Thanks!

Slide 39: Finally

Finally: Have fun! Don't be disappointed when you lose an auction. There will always be more items to look at and bid on.

Thanks for your attention. We covered a lot of ground in this class. All of the tips and procedures we discussed are in your handouts. Take a look at them and the online auction sites and maybe give it a try.

Are there any questions?

Module 12
Picturing the Digital
Camera Revolution

INTRODUCTION

How many of your libraries have added a digital camera to your arsenal of technological equipment? How many of your users have purchased a digital camera for the family at Christmas or before holiday time? Digital imaging is one of the newest HOT things in the world of technology and the Internet. If your library users have questions about cameras and what can be done with them, this module will help them.

The advent of the Web as a means to easily display and send images as attachments to e-mail messages has set the stage for the digital camera revolution. Once pricey and difficult to use, inexpensive, friendly models are being marketed aggressively and the serious "photo bug" has a wider choice of higher-end models with more professional features.

Web sites specializing in storing photos and offering high-quality prints and gift ideas are prominent these days, including Ofoto, PhotoPoint, and Sony's ImageStation. Magazines such as *Digital Camera, Digital Photographer, Sony Style*, and more highlight and promote this exciting new medium.

A NOTE ABOUT THE MODULE

This is the most image-intensive module in the *Toolkit*. Weighing in at a whopping 10 megs, it may be cumbersome to work with. The size results from the inclusion of over 20 digital photos taken with my Sony Mavica FD95 at my home in Mishawaka, Indiana; in Traverse City, Michigan; and on holiday in various parts of the United States.

Feel free to copy the module to your hard drive or other large storage media and edit it as needed. Insert some of your own photographs in place of mine. Have you documented the change of seasons in your town? At your library? Use those photos instead to give the module that local feel.

All of the images used can also be found in a directory on the CD-ROM and can be used as you see fit.

WORKSHOP ATTENDEES WILL GAIN:

1. An understanding of how a digital camera works, what features are available, and what types of storage solutions are offered by camera makers.
2. An overview of points to consider when buying a digital camera: cost, pixels, speed, features, and so on.
3. An overview of Web sites that offer storage, printing, and value-added services for digital photographers.

TIPS FOR PRESENTING THIS MODULE

- This module begins with a few slides in automatic slide show mode. They are timed to be about 4 to 5 seconds each. Adjust the timings as needed.
- Use your library's camera if possible to demonstrate during or after the presentation. I have taken pictures of my audience or the room beforehand and then displayed them for the group. Weather or current events make an interesting demonstration: I've used photos of the Midwest's winter of 2000 and the destruction of a local factory complex by implosion to demonstrate my camera.
- Invite participants to bring their digital cameras for a brief "show and tell." This worked very well when I presented this class in Nappanee, Indiana, in spring 2001. I asked each person who had brought their camera to tell the group about it and what they used the camera for.
- Keep this module current by keeping current with digital camera innovations: increased pixel capacities, new storage media, new innovations, and so on.
- Go live on the Web and demonstrate ofoto.com or a similar image storage site.
- Order a few prints from one of the storage sites in advance to have on hand to pass around the group.

MODULE 12—PICTURING THE DIGITAL CAMERA REVOLUTION— SCRIPT

Slide 1: Introduction

<Introduce yourself and your helper if you have one. Tell the group that you will be using a presentation program called PowerPoint to present the programme.>

Welcome to the class on **digital cameras**. Let's start with a short automated slide show to introduce our subject.

<Slides 2 to 10 are for the slide show that opens the session.>

holiday memories

travel snapshots

a beloved friend

a family event

the new car

And much, much more!

Slide 11: Digital Cameras

Here's our plan for the class. We'll discuss exactly what a digital camera is. We'll look a little bit at the techie stuff that makes it work. I'll define some terms that will help you understand the ins and outs of taking digital pictures.

We'll look at the benefits of digital photography as well as some of the drawbacks. Then we'll talk about purchasing a camera and what you can do with the pictures you take.

Digital Cameras

- What are digital cameras?
- What are the benefits of digital photography?
- What should I look for when purchasing?
- What can I do with my photos

Slide 12: Digital Cameras

Digital cameras are very popular right now. Who owns one?

<Allow audience to respond.>

Who has friends or relatives who own a digital camera?

<Allow audience to respond.>

Digital Cameras

- Increasingly popular
  - 4.5 million cameras sold in 2000
  - 8 million will be sold in 2001
- Prices falling rapidly

Who has received a picture via e-mail that someone took with a digital camera?

<Allow audience to respond.>

Digital cameras or digicams have certainly become increasingly popular. The January 2001 issue *of Kiplinger's Personal Finance Magazine* reports that almost double the number of digital cameras sold in 2000 will be sold in 2001.

The article also predicts that prices will fall rapidly for many consumer technology items. A digital camera that takes high-quality pictures that sold for £500 in 1999 may drop to around £150.

So if you're thinking about joining the digital camera revolution, the next few months may be a good time to do so.

What are Digital Cameras?

- Instead of film, camera sensors record light and colour digitally on storage media.
- Charge-Coupled Device - CCD
- Quality is stated in pixel size.

Slide 13: What are Digital Cameras?

So how do these things work? Instead of using film, the digital camera's sensors record light and colour digitally on storage media. The CCD—**Charge-Coupled Device**—is the sensor that records the image. The CCD is like the reader or scanner that grabs an image through the lens and writes it in digital format to a storage disk.

Quality for cameras and pictures is expressed in **pixel** size. Have you heard someone say she just bought a 3.1 megapixel camera? That's the number of pixels found on the CCD.

What are Pixels?

- The building blocks of a digital photograph
- Picture Element = Pixel

1200

1600 X 1200=
1,920,000 pixels

1600

Slide 14: What are Pixels?

What are pixels then? They are the building blocks of a digital photograph. Pixel is short for picture element. That's the little dots that make up the picture. The CCD has a certain number of pixels. Here's a diagram of a CCD that is 1600 pixels wide by 1200 pixels high. That's almost two million pixels creating the digital image.

Slide 15: More about Pixels

When a camera has one million pixels, it's called a **megapixel** camera. A camera with over three million pixels is a three-megapixel camera. Don't worry about all of this CCD stuff; just remember that the higher the number of pixels, the better the image.

Slide 16: How many pixels do I need?

In fact, a three- or four megapixel digital camera rivals the images you can capture with a regular 35mm camera. That means that when you print you can enlarge up to 8X10 or possibly 11X14 print size and still see sharp, clear images.

The highest number of pixels I've seen recently is 41 for new cameras.

<Adjust this number as needed.>

Slide 17: Image Comparison

Here's a comparison of the same picture taken with a digital camera at the lowest quality and at the highest quality. Notice the sharpness and details of the larger image. That image, however, uses more storage space on your recording media.

Slide 18: 3 Megapixel Cameras

Here's another photo, taken with pixel quality that would allow us to reprint as an 8X10.

Any questions?

<Allow audience to respond.>

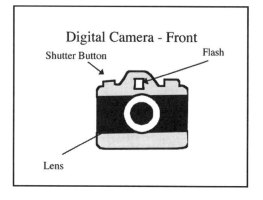

Slide 19: Digital Camera Brands

There are many brands of cameras to choose from. Here's a few of the big names, some of the most popular digital camera manufacturers today.

No matter what brand you purchase, the features and details of the camera are pretty much the same.

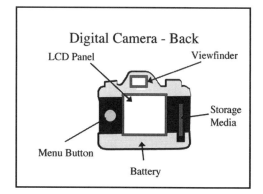

Slide 20: Digital Camera Front

For example, here's the front of a typical digital camera. No matter what brand you buy, the camera will have a lens for focusing and capturing the image, a shutter button to press to take the picture, and probably a built-in flash.

Slide 21: Digital Camera Back

The back of the camera is a little more detailed. You'll find a viewfinder that works just like a regular 35mm camera, a slot to install the battery or batteries, and a few extra features that regular cameras do not have.

The LCD panel is like an electronic viewfinder. LCD stands for **Liquid Crystal Display**. Have you noticed people at tourist spots standing with their cameras held out in front of them? They are probably looking at their LCD to frame their shot instead of at the optical viewfinder.

<I usually tell a story about visiting the Jefferson Memorial in Washington, D.C., and realizing I was lined up with a group of other people all shooting the cherry blossoms with our digital cameras: arms stretched out in front of us, clutching various makes and models of digital cameras, and scrutinizing the LCD.>

The LCD also allows you to view a picture after you have captured it from the storage media in the camera. You could call it instant gratification—getting to see the picture you snapped immediately.

The **storage media** probably slides into the side or back of the camera. Different brands of cameras use different types of storage media. We'll talk about storage in just a few minutes.

Finally, there will be a **menu button** or buttons of some type that allow you to choose the options for the camera, like special effects, image size, and exposure times. Some cameras will have many more features than others so they may have more buttons or menu choices. The menu will display on the LCD as you work with the camera.

Slide 22: What are the benefits of digital photography?

Now we know a little bit about how the digital camera works. Next, let's look at the benefits of digital photography.

Using a digital camera is a relatively low-cost endeavour. After the purchase of the camera and possibly some accessories like extra storage media and batteries, the cost to use the camera is virtually nil. There is no film to purchase or developing to pay for. If you print your pictures with your colour printer, you might go through toner cartridges rather quickly and use up paper, but the cost per picture is very low.

Shooting with a digital camera is also environmentally friendly. You are not consuming rolls and rolls of film, metal canisters, little plastic storage cylinders and other packaging, or chemicals used for developing.

As I mentioned earlier, with a digital camera you can immediately view your images. If you don't like

What are the benefits of digital photography?
- Low cost
- Environmentally friendly
- Chance to reshoot/delete "duds"
- Easily shared, archived, and used

the shot you snapped of the family at the reunion—maybe cousin Eddie was making a face—you can take another. You can also delete images you decide you do not want, freeing up space on your media for those pictures you do.

Images you capture can be easily shared and archived. You can attach an image to an e-mail message. You can store images on floppy disk, your hard drive, or on recordable CD. You can manipulate them in graphics programs and use them in your computer creations, such as newsletters, reports, or fliers.

Slide 23: But what about the drawbacks?

What about the drawbacks of using a digital camera?

With some cameras, there can be a long lag time when shooting. You may have to wait between three and ten seconds for an image to write to the media before you can take another photo. That could be frustrating if you are trying to capture the action of a football game or the launch of the space shuttle.

Printing images on your own printer can be costly. Factor in the wear and tear on your printer, the cost of colour cartridges and photo paper, and you may find it's not the most cost-effective way to get prints of your digital images. And the quality of the prints may not be as high as you'd like, depending on the printer's capabilities. Not everyone you know has a computer so it might be difficult to share images with them. And if you're interested in digital cameras but do not have a computer, you may have to purchase one or use a friend or relative's machine.

Any questions?

<Allow audience to respond.>

But what about the drawbacks?

- Slow lag time when shooting
- Printing images yourself can be costly
- Not everyone has a computer

Slide 24: Digital Camera Buying Tips

If you're ready to buy, though, here's a list of things to consider when going out to look at all of the choices available at the local electronics store.

Let's go through these one by one.

> Digital Camera Buying Tips
>
> - Types of use
> - Type of storage media
> - Connectivity
> - Battery type
> - Lens strength
> - Bells and whistles
> - Price

Slide 25: How will you use your camera?

How will you use your camera? Depending on your needs, you may need only a standard digital camera. If you're looking for more high-end features and quality, there are many high-end models available.

For Web pages, viewing on home computers, and for e-mailing to relatives and friends, a standard camera much like a conventional "point and shoot" film camera would be fine. This might possibly be a camera with a one-megapixel CCD.

The more uses you have for the camera, the more features and quality you may want. Family holidays, sports events, or action shots are best recorded by a more advanced camera. You might want to consider features like autofocus and different exposure programs to get the most out of the camera. Autofocus is popular in many digicams. With autofocus, the camera will capture the image when it's in focus, preventing the blurry or shaky quality of some shots.

If you are ready to dive in and replace your standard film camera, you might look for the most pixels and features you can afford.

> How will you use your camera?
>
> - Web pages, computers, and online only
> - Family events and holidays
> - Sports and action events
> - Replacement for a standard 35mm camera
>
>

What type of storage?

- Floppy disk
- SmartMedia or Compact Flash card
- Memory Stick from Sony
- 4MB / 8MB / 32MB / 64MB / 128MB

Slide 26: What type of storage?

Consider what type of storage media to use for digital images. There are four distinct options for storage right now in the digital camera arena: the regular floppy disk, **Compact Flash** media, **SmartMedia**, and the **Memory Stick** from Sony.

Most cameras will use either the Flash or SmartMedia cards. With your camera purchase you may get a card reader that plugs into your computer to transfer pictures. Or the card will plug into your PC with an adaptor. Many Kodak cameras come with a card reader and adaptor. These cards are about the size of a matchbook and can hold as much as 200 megs of images, depending on the size of the card.

Sony cameras use a regular floppy disk or the Sony Memory Stick. A Memory Stick can hold 4, 8, 32, or 64 meg of pictures. It's a little smaller than a stick of gum.

All of these storage media are available in various sizes. Here's a hint: You may want to own two or three medium-sized cards instead of one really large card. If you lost the one large card, you'd lose all of your pictures.

How will you connect?

- Disk drive
- Card reader
- USB cable connection w/software
- New technologies - CDR, etc.

Slide 27: How will you connect?

How will you connect to your computer to transfer the images? You can insert a floppy into your PC's disk drive or connect a card reader. USB cable connections require the addition of software drivers to transfer images via the Universal Serial Bus, which has become a standard peripheral connection in most new computers.

Newer technologies are changing connection and transfer methods as well. In the summer of 2000, Sony released a digital camera that writes images to a three-inch **CD recorder** built into the body of the camera. There are no cables to connect, cards to insert, or software to load. The little CDR is read by any computer with a CD-ROM drive. This improves the ease with which we can share pictures and archive our images.

Slide 28: What type of battery?

Batteries are also a consideration when selecting a digital camera. Some cameras can be energy hogs—using up batteries very quickly. There are several types of batteries to choose from.

The **Lithium Ion battery** is used in some digital cameras. It is long-lasting and easily rechargeable. One type of these is called the **InfoLithium**. These batteries provide a readout of the remaining battery time in minutes on the LCD screen.

Nickel Metal Hydride or NiMH are environmentally friendly batteries used in many brands of digital cameras.

Some cameras take AA-size batteries just like many of our other electronic devices. A rechargeable AA is a good selection for this type of camera because batteries can be depleted quickly by lots of flash photography, longer exposures, and higher image quality.

Most cameras also come with a power supply for charging the lithium or NiMH batteries or for use with the camera. If you were shooting a lot of indoor scenes with your camera on a tripod—like the family Christmas card—you could plug your camera into the power supply and save battery time.

What type of battery?

- Lithium Ion
- Nickel Metal Hydride - NiMH
- Rechargable AAs
- Power Supply

Slide 29: What type of lens?

If you are an avid photographer, you might consider the size of the lens on the camera as an important factor for purchase. The numbers here reflect the power of the lens to zoom in on a subject. The higher the number, the closer you can zoom in on your subject.

For example, here's the Space Needle in Seattle. And beside it is a zoom in at ten times strength to capture the observation deck.

Some cameras will boost the lens strength with a digital zoom feature. Digital zoom is an electronic enlargement done inside the camera. Using digital zoom results in some loss of pixel quality.

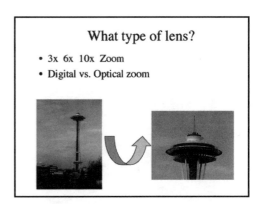

What type of lens?

- 3x 6x 10x Zoom
- Digital vs. Optical zoom

The Bells and Whistles

- Program settings and ISO equivalents
- Self-timer
- Movie mode
- Special effects

Slide 30: The Bells and Whistles

You may want to consider what bells and whistles come with your camera. What snazzy things can it do? What extras make it really cool to use?

These features include program settings and ISO equivalents. These allow us to set the camera on "Night Mode" for certain pictures or emulate the results one might get with 400-speed film.

A self-timer is invaluable as well for taking pictures you want to be in as well. Most will count down about ten seconds, then capture the image. Some models take this a step further and come with a remote control for snapping pictures.

Movie mode allows us to record not a still image but a moving one. I may be riding a double-decker bus in England and want to capture the feeling of moving through the streets as buildings go by. I could set my camera to this mode and record a small movie that I can play back and share with others. The quality is nowhere near that of video cameras or the newer digital video cameras, but it is a fun option to have.

Then there are the special effects. You may have heard someone say that his digital camera has some cool special effects. Those effects can create some great images. For example—

Special Effects - Low Light

Slide 31: Special Effects—Low Light

Here is a lake in northern Michigan at night shot in the low light mode. The shutter stays open longer and captures the light of the candles on the pier and the blues our eyes do not see.

Slide 32: Special Effects—B&W

Here's a nature shot done in black and white.

Slide 33: Special Effects—Sepia

This shot uses the sepia mode to make the picture look old or antique. Sepia uses varying shades of brown and yellow to give that old-fashioned appearance.

Slide 34: Special Effects—Negative

Here's the negative special effect—great for creative uses on Web sites or in photo projects.

Slide 35: Special Effects—Solarize

And here is the solarize feature that overenhances colours.

Price

- Be sure to compare prices carefully.
- Prices are falling all the time.

Slide 36: Price

Of course, the most important factor that will influence your purchasing decision is the price of the camera. Remember that prices are falling every day as digital cameras become more and more popular and new models are introduced.

My suggestion: Just like with pixel size, go for the most features and bells and whistles you can afford. You'll want to use them as you get more comfortable with the camera. You may not need the super high-end model. You might, however, be better served by a middle-range camera that you grow into instead of one that has so few features or pixels that you are ready for a new one a week after you bring it home.

What can I do with my photos?

- Download, display, and print on your PC
- E-mail to friends and relatives
- Manipulate with software
- Incorporate into Web pages
- Archive on CDR
- Upload to Web sites to print and store

Slide 37: What can I do with my photos?

You've bought your camera and you've started shooting digital pictures. You capture the next family event. You follow Rover around the backyard doing a canine photo study. You take your camera on holiday and capture all the sights of the National Parks. What can you do with the pictures you've taken?

You can download and display them on your PC. With a colour printer and photo paper you can make your own prints. You can e-mail your favourites to friends and relatives.

If you are building a Web site, you can incorporate images into the pages. To do this you may also be pulling them into image manipulation software to edit and enhance them. Most cameras include software to help you manipulate and have fun with your images. PhotoDeluxe from Adobe is one such program. Adobe PhotoShop is the high-end cousin of PhotoDeluxe. It's used by many high-end graphic firms.

You can archive your photos on CDR. You might even give CDs of family photos to your relatives as gifts.

You can also upload your pictures to Web sites for printing and storage. Let's talk a bit about these sites.

Slide 38: Photo-Hosting Web Sites

Photo-hosting Web sites are becoming more prevalent on the Internet with the digital camera explosion. They allow you to upload, organize, share, and print your pictures. Hosting is free or a minimal charge at some sites. Printing is usually a small expense considering you didn't buy film or pay for developing. You might upload 50 vacation photos and then choose 20 to order as 4X6 prints. Those prints are shipped out to you in a mailer, usually very quickly.

These sites allow you to share galleries of your images with others via e-mail. If I share the gallery of my holiday pictures, my friends receive an e-mail directing them to the Web site to look at the photos. My friends can even order prints of my pictures and add comments!

These sites offer perks and specials throughout the year, like deals on photo Christmas cards and frames.

Photo-Hosting Web Sites

- Allow FREE storage of your photos
- Offer printing and shipping of photos
- Allow shared galleries
- Offer perks and specials throughout the year

Slide 39: Photo-Hosting Web Sites

Here are a few of the many photo sites available. Each has unique features and deals. Some will give you free prints for joining. Take a look at them next time you are surfing the Web.

Photo-Hosting Web Sites

- www.dotphoto.com
- www.eframes.com
- www.net-album.net
- www.ofoto.com
- www.photopoint.com
- www.shutterfly.com
- www.zing.com

Slide 40: www.ofoto.com

Let's look at one of these a little more closely to give you an idea of how they work.

This is Ofoto's front page. It offers image storage, sharing, printing, and the opportunity to take advantage of extras like free image manipulation software and an online shop devoted to frames for your pictures.

Slide 41: Galleries at Ofoto

Here's a sample account at Ofoto. Notice each gallery has a name and a representative image. There are links for sharing and uploading images, as well as other features.

Slide 42: Ordering Prints at Ofoto

Here is the page for ordering prints. I might select a few of them and then click on the "Order Prints Now" button. A series of pages follow, confirming my selections and finalizing the order. In a few days, I receive my prints in the mail.

Please take a look at any of the image-hosting sites listed in your handout and you'll see similar features.

Slide 43: Thanks!

Thanks for you attention. We have covered a lot of ground. Are there any questions about digital cameras?

References/Endnotes

SCREENSHOTS USED BY PERMISSION

British Education Communication and Technology agency *www.becta.org.uk/technology/ safetyseminar/index.html*

BUBL Information Service *http://bubl.ac.uk*

Castle in the Country *www.castleinthecountry.com*

Doc Pierce's *www.docpierces.com*

eBay™ *www.ebay.com*

Fischoff National Chamber Music Association *www.fischoff.org*

Google *www.google.com*

Jake's Page *tesla.sjcpl.lib.in.us/Jake/Jake.html*

Ofoto *www.ofoto.com*

Parliamentary Education Unit, "Explore Parliament" *http://parliament.eduweb.co.uk*

SafeKids *www.safekids.com*

UK Net Guide *www.ukgovernmentguide.co.uk*

Yahoo! *www.yahoo.com*

PREFACE

For a detailed examination of the origins of Internet use at SJCPL, please see "The Public Library in Transition: Paradigm Shifts Toward the New Millennium," by SJCPL Director Donald Napoli, published in *The Evolving Virtual Library II*, edited by Laverna Saunders (Information Today, 1999).

SEARCHING THE WORLD WIDE WEB

Snider, Mike. 2000. "More Useless Info: 2 Billion Web Pages." *USA Today*, 11 July 2000, 3D.

EVALUATING WEB SITES

Etkin, Cindy. *Critically Evaluating Web Resources* available at *www.tametheweb.com/ evalweb/web-eval.htm*

Please see the *Web Evaluation Bibliography* available at *www.lib.vt.edu/research/libinst/ evalbiblio.html*

SHOPPING THE WORLD WIDE WEB—THE INTERNET CONSUMER GUIDE

Berman, Dennis K., and Ben Elgin. 2001. "Amazon and Yahoo!: All that Glitters . . . " *Business Week*, 8 January 2001, 38.

"Best Stuff to Buy Online Chart." *Consumer Reports*, December 2000.

Holiday Shopping Lags. PC Data Online (January 2, 2001) Available at: *www.pcdataonline.com/press/pcdo010201.asp*

EXPLORING INTERNET VIDEO AND AUDIO

Humphrey, Jeff. 2000. *Internet Audio*. INCOLSA Handout. E-mail Jeff at *jeff@incolsa.net*

CHATTING ON THE INTERNET

Truxall, Richard. 1998. *Chatting Up a Storm*. (Presentation at American Library Association annual meeting.) Available at: *www.truxall.com*

SURFING SAFE! CHILDREN AND THEIR PARENTS ON THE WORLD WIDE WEB

American Library Association. *Great Sites!* (2001) Available at: *www.ala.org/parentspage/greatsites*

American Library Association. *Librarian's Guide to Cyberspace for Parents and Kids*. (2001) Available at: *www.ala.org/parentspage/greatsites/guide.html*

Magid, Larry. *Child Safety on the Information Highway*. (2001) Available at: *www.safekids.com/*

Sesame Workshop. *Family Tech Tips*. (2001) Available at: *www.sesameworkshop.org/parents/techtips*

SELLING AND SAVING: EXPLORING WWW AUCTIONS

ALI Music Corporation. *100 Top Auction Sites*. (2001) Available at: *www.100topauctionsites.com/*

PICTURING THE DIGITAL CAMERA REVOLUTION

Armstrong, Larry. "Digital Cameras Are Coming into Focus." *Business Week*, 4 December 2000, 160.

Roha, Ronaleen R. "Tech: Cooler, Faster, Better." *Kiplinger's Personal Finance Magazine* 55, no.1 (January 2001): 111.

Index

About the Author

Michael T. Stephens is the Networked Resources Training Specialist at the St. Joseph County Public Library in South Bend, Indiana. He received his MLS from Indiana University in 1995.

Stephens designs and instructs ongoing staff training sessions as well as public classes on various topics related to the Internet, electronic databases, and emerging technologies in information. His independent training, Web design, and consulting venture (*www.tametheweb.com*) is utilized by librarians and other professionals. He has taught library staff sessions and public classes for many northern Indiana libraries.

Stephens has presented programmes at various regional locations and at the Indiana Library Federation annual meeting since 1997. In July 2000, Stephens presented a "Bibliographic Instruction for the New Age" programme at the Federal Library Information Center Committee (FLICC) Reference Workshop at the Library of Congress in Washington, D.C. He has also made major presentations at The Computers in Libraries conferences of both 2000 and 2001.

ABOUT THE ADAPTER

Phil Bradley is an information professional who has worked extensively with and on the Internet for eight years. He is an Internet trainer who has run courses for The Library Association, TFPL, Aslib, UKOLUG, The Greater London Authority and the British Council among others. He writes, designs and maintains Web sites for many different clients.

Phil also speaks at conferences, such as Online and UKOLUG, and exhibitions in the UK and abroad on Internet-related matters.

Finally, he is also an author, having published several Internet-related titles, including *The Advanced Internet Searcher's Handbook*, published by Library Association Publishing.